JOB DESCRIPTIONS
IN MARKETING MANAGEMENT

AMA RESEARCH STUDY 94

JOB DESCRIPTIONS
IN MARKETING MANAGEMENT

JoAnn Sperling

AMERICAN MANAGEMENT ASSOCIATION, INC.

About This Report

WHY TAKE THE TIME to write a job description?

Marketing managers report that, not only is it worth the time, but the job description process also is an investment in the future. Preparation of a job description gives a chance for thoughtful discussion of a man's job and its priorities. A well-thought-out, up-to-date job description spells out duties, responsibilities, and limits of authority of a particular position; helps other departments to understand the job; serves as a basis for setting performance standards and objectives; is used to identify management development needs. It assists corporate management in obtaining data for job classification and salary administration and in recruiting managers for similar positions. It is a valuable source of informational input when revisions in organization structure are being considered.

Since the publication of AMA's *Defining the Manager's Job* in 1958 and of *Managerial Job Descriptions in Manufacturing* in 1964, the AMA Research and Information Service has received increasing demands for marketing job descriptions. *Job Descriptions in Marketing Management* has been compiled to meet this need.

Managers mapping out a new marketing structure or reorganizing or updating an existing one will find job descriptions in this study covering a wide range of marketing positions: advertising, market research, sales, product planning, marketing administration, marketing services, customer services, as well as top marketing management. Complete sets of marketing department job descriptions for the marketing departments of a consumer-oriented and an industrial company are included to show the interrelations of the positions.

Many marketing executives contacted in the AMA survey on which this report is based stated that accurate and realistic job descriptions are necessary to the smooth operation of any professionally

5

managed organization. The report describes their views and experiences regarding the uses to which job descriptions are put in their organizations, the range of responsibilities covered, and the relationships between different marketing functions shown in the descriptions. These executives also supplied data on the frequency of job description review and expressed their opinions on the future use of job descriptions in their organizations.

To assist the executive about to embark on a job description program, the report analyzes various aspects of job description format. The 587 marketing job descriptions submitted in the course of the research were studied for length of the job description, date it was written and approved, the title of the document, length and content of items appearing in the job description, method of authority coverage, and the percentage of job descriptions containing job specifications.

JoAnn Sperling, a Research Associate at the American Management Association, conducted the research for this study. Miss Sperling joined AMA in 1961 and assumed her present position in 1967. A graduate of Fairleigh Dickinson University, she has attended many AMA activities, and was graduated from its Management Course in June 1968. She has written several articles for *Management News* and has compiled editions of AMA's *Directory of Consultant Members* and the *Ten-Year Index of AMA Publications* and its supplements.

JOHN W. ENELL
Vice President for Research

Contents

Tables

Exhibits

A Handbook of Managerial Job Descriptions in Marketing

1. Overview of the Survey Findings

ACCURATE AND REALISTIC JOB DESCRIPTIONS are necessary to the smooth operation of any professionally managed corporation, in the opinion of many marketing executives who were consulted in this AMA survey on the use and content of job descriptions in marketing management.

Because of the atmosphere of constant change in the marketing area, job descriptions are of continuing importance. The job description is the cornerstone of job definition and scope. Solid foundations must be built so that the individual may clearly perceive his responsibilities and comprehend his relationships, both internal and external; thus his superiors will be able to relate his job to the total sphere of the marketing activity. J. D. Batten has pointed out the urgency of this analysis and evaluation:

> Every marketing function should be isolated, defined, and evaluated in terms of its contribution to marketing objectives. The relative importance of functions is constantly changing. . . . All such factors should have a pronounced effect upon the assignment of responsibility.*

This ever changing climate in marketing makes great demands on individual performance—specifically, it requires optimum individual results. Companies that adhere to a sound marketing concept find that a results-oriented approach based on performance standards provides an accurate measurement of individual contribution. The development of effective performance standards, then, is contingent on the company's job description program. A great deal of interest

---

*J. D. Batten, *Developing a Tough-Minded Climate . . . for Results*, American Management Association, New York, 1965, p. 60.

in job description programs has been evident in recent years, as indicated by repeated inquiries received by the American Management Association's Research and Information Service regarding broad as well as specific details of job description programs for marketing management.

The primary instrument used in gathering information about marketing job descriptions for this study was a survey that the American Management Association mailed to marketing and personnel executives in 576 companies. Five hundred and eighty-seven sample job descriptions were received, in addition to data supplied by each company about its job description program.

On the basis of an analysis of the usable responses to this survey, several conclusions relative to the effective use of job descriptions for marketing positions can be drawn:

- Clarification of job responsibilities was cited by 72 percent of the responding companies (80 of 111) as the primary purpose of the job description in their marketing organizations.

- The use of the job description to set the basis for performance appraisal was mentioned as the primary purpose by 46 percent (51 of 111) of the companies.

- In 32 percent of the companies (35 of 111) participants believe that the most meaningful purpose of the job description is to clarify jobs for the benefit of other company divisions.

- Relationships with operational, nonmarketing departments of companies are spelled out in 53 percent of the marketing job descriptions (59 of 111).

- In 29 percent of the companies (27 of 94 responses), participants state that job descriptions serve primarily to *indicate* rather than define job responsibilities; however, in 44 companies (47 percent) executives state that job descriptions serve specifically to *describe* or define job duties in detail.

- Planning is the most frequently described type of management activity in the job descriptions of 92 percent of the participating companies (83 of 90).

- In 91 percent of the companies (81 of 89), the executives surveyed consult their job descriptions at least once a year,

(*Text continues on page 16.*)

BASIS OF THE RESEARCH

Since the publication by the American Management Association of *Defining the Manager's Job* 11 years ago, AMA's Research and Information Service and Library have received a steadily increasing number of requests for marketing job descriptions. *Job Descriptions in Marketing Management* has been compiled to meet this need. Material for the study was obtained from a mail survey and questionnaire sent to 576 companies in June 1966 and updated during July and August 1968.

The companies were selected from the 1965 *Fortune Directory of the 500 Largest U.S. Industrial Corporations* and from the American Management Association's membership files of individuals and companies enrolled in its Marketing Division.

A four-page questionnaire was sent to the chief marketing executive in each company to obtain information regarding the purposes and extent of use of job descriptions, primary responsibilities covered, frequency of review, responsibility for the program, and predictions on future use of the job description. A letter was also sent to 430 personnel vice presidents and personnel managers, 370 of whom were from the same firms as the marketing executives surveyed, requesting samples of their marketing job descriptions.

The report is based on questionnaire responses from 111 companies and on 587 specimen marketing job descriptions submitted by 190 participating companies, as well as by the participants in several AMA Marketing Division programs. Each job description or quote used is published with the consent of the participating company.

Three-fourths of the report is devoted to a collection of 48 sample job descriptions showing a wide range of marketing positions: advertising, market research, sales, product planning, marketing administration, marketing services, and customer service. Also included are sets of marketing department job descriptions for two companies. The balance of the report analyzes the job descriptions submitted for this survey and covers the various purposes for which these guides are used, the range of responsibilities described, the relationships between different marketing functions, frequency of review, and future uses.

Additional information was gathered from an examination of literature and discussions with speakers participating in AMA Marketing Division programs.

and 47 percent of the companies (42 of 89) consult their descriptions every several months.

- Responsibility for writing the initial job description is left entirely to the jobholder in 20 percent (19 of 94) of the responding organizations. In 18 companies the superior alone has the responsibility, and in 17 organizations a company specialist prepares the initial document.
- In 45 percent of the companies (42 of 94), executives believe that job descriptions will remain in their present form for at least the next five years; in 55 percent (52 companies), participants foresee changes in the format or principal use of job descriptions within the next five years.

Format, the general organization or arrangement of job descriptions, was also analyzed as a basic part of the research process for this study.

The descriptions submitted were examined for data on their length, the dates they were written and approved, the titles of the documents, the length and content of the items appearing in the job descriptions, the method for assigning scope of authority, the percentage of job descriptions containing job specifications, and other features. Highlighting some of the information uncovered are the following:

- Of the 587 job descriptions, 19 percent (112) are one page long; 42 percent (247) two pages; 21 percent (125) three pages; and only 4 percent (20) fill more than six pages.
- In 98 percent (574), the first item to appear on the job description is a job summary.
- Limits of authority are not often outlined in marketing job descriptions; only 24 percent (143) mention restrictions on or limits to authority.
- Only 22 percent (127) show the span of control exercised by the jobholder.
- Job specifications are contained in 14 percent (80) of the descriptions.

2. Content, Scope, and Use of the Job Description

THE JOB DESCRIPTION is the instrument for delineation of job responsibility. At the same time, it may indicate the degree of authority exercised and the relationships necessary to carry out the business of an individual job.

Detailed Versus Broad Approach

DISCUSSIONS MAY CONTINUE indefinitely on the merits of a detailed job description versus a broad outline of responsibilities. Research for this study indicates that companies advance strong cases for both methods; but, because of the diversity of responding organizations, especially within marketing groups, many variations of each approach are evident.

Of the 48 companies that express an opinion, 28 prefer the detailed type of description, and 20 the general approach.

This typical statement defines the elements that one of the respondents considers essential to a job description:

> A good position description must contain the importance of the work in terms of impact on operations; the mental application required of the incumbent in planning, problem solving, and making decisions; and the total "know-how" required to perform the position. In addition, the scope of responsibility and decision-making authority should be clearly indicated. A position description that does not have that is inadequate. [A mining company]

Another respondent presented a modified version of this approach:

> The job changes somewhat with the man in it. . . . Too trite or narrow a description is really meaningless—actually allows wide margin of performance judgment. A good . . . description should "fit the man" in the job and should define not only his responsibilities, objectives, and authority, but also his relations with others. [An automobile and aircraft accessory manufacturer]

The opposite point of view was also represented by a data processing equipment manufacturer: "A good job description at the executive level avoids specific details and permits the broadest possible latitude for achieving objectives."

One of the shortest lists of requirements came from a clothing manufacturer: "[The] job description should be broad enough to permit growth, flexible enough to permit imagination, clear enough to define authority."

SCOPE OF INDIVIDUAL JOB DESCRIPTION COVERAGE

Either job description responsibilities can be indicated—that is, job duties outlined with little or no further explanation—or responsibilities can be described or shown in detail.

The following excerpt from a description of the duties of the manager–market and economic research of a mining company illustrates the depth of coverage that some companies employ:

MANAGER–MARKET AND ECONOMIC RESEARCH

Establishes and conducts a program of market research and analysis designed to ascertain and evaluate industry and general economic trends, . . . supply and demand balances, market potentials, competitors' market positions, and company's present and potential share of the . . . market, on a worldwide basis. This includes the compilation, analysis, and evaluation of:

a. Information about competitors' activities and plans;
b. Competitors' estimated and company's current and forecast production costs;
c. General economic and business trend information having direct and indirect bearing on the company's product markets and consumption;
d. Possible effect of international events and local, national, and worldwide political developments on markets and consumption;
e. Possible effect of variables associated with labor contract negotiations;
f. Product price trends;

g. Statistics and trends relating to market size and territorial potentials by product and product categories;

h. . . . sales records and trends;

i. Company's sales costs.

Organizations that indicate job responsibilities broadly (27 responses—29 percent of the total 94 responding to the question) usually keep their descriptions brief and general in scope. For example, following is the job description for the regional marketing manager of one oil company; it contains fewer than a hundred words.

Province: Activities of districts within the assigned territory.

Place in Organization: Reports to Vice President, Marketing Region.

Personnel Supervised: State Manager (Western Region only); District Managers.

Specific Responsibilities:

1. Supervise the management of assigned districts.

2. Establish specific marketing objectives; approve plans for the accomplishment of these objectives and measurements of performance for districts supervised.

3. When designated, act for the Region Vice President during his absence or unavailability.

PATTERNS OF FUNCTION COVERAGE

Participating companies also defined which major management functions—planning, reporting, budget control, decision making, delegation of authority, appraisal, approval authority, approval of subordinates' salaries, joint responsibility—are covered in their marketing job descriptions. For a complete listing of their views, see Table 1.

Certain patterns emerge from these data. The sharp focus on planning responsibility in job descriptions reflects both the increasing sophistication of marketing operations throughout the United States and their emphasis on professional management techniques.

The failure of many respondents to mention approval of subordinates' salaries should not be construed as indicating that this responsibility is not given proper weight in the marketing management process; to the contrary, this function apparently is considered an

TABLE 1.   *Extent to Which Job Responsibilities Are Indicated or Described in Job Descriptions, in 90 Companies*

MANAGEMENT FUNCTION FOR WHICH JOB DESCRIPTION INDICATES OR DESCRIBES RESPONSIBILITY	COMPANIES	PERCENT
Planning	83	92
Reporting	74	82
Budget Control	67	74
Decision Making	63	70
Delegation of Authority	59	66
Appraisal	54	60
Approval Authority	54	60
Approval of Subordinates' Salaries	37	41
Joint Responsibility	35	39

integral part of marketing management and, as such, is simply taken for granted.

Delegation of authority, although mentioned in most job descriptions, is not always spelled out. This activity is rated high in 66 percent of the total mentions (59 companies).

For example, the description of delegation of authority may take the form of an outline, such as this one from a pharmaceutical distributor: "[The executive] may delegate to the assistants under his direction appropriate portions of his responsibilities, together with proportionate authority for their fulfillment, but he may not delegate or relinquish his overall responsibility for results or any portion of his accountability."

The number of executives who stated that the management functions are described in detail in their job descriptions was twice as large as the number who reported that these responsibilities are merely indicated. There was a slightly greater tendency for executives to state, however, that the decision making responsibility is described in detail even though other job responsibilities may be only indicated.

Frequency of Review

IN MOST OF THE RESPONDING COMPANIES, job descriptions are consulted and reviewed rather frequently by the incumbent, his superior, or other members of the organization.

When the respondents were asked to pinpoint the most recent occasion on which they had consulted their job descriptions, the following data emerged:

- Almost half the participants, 47 percent (42 of 89), stated that they had consulted their job descriptions at least once during the preceding several months.
- Twenty-seven percent (24 executives) had consulted their job descriptions during the month preceding the survey.
- Seventeen percent (15 executives) had reviewed their descriptions at least once during the preceding year.
- Only 9 percent (eight executives) could not remember when they had last reviewed their job descriptions.

Often, however, the reasons for consultation of the job description are not the same as the stated primary purposes of the description.

This is not new. To quote C. L. Bennet, in *Defining the Manager's Job* (American Management Association, 1958): "Current uses made by a company of its managerial position descriptions often bear little relationship to those originally envisioned when the programs first started. . . . In fact, 'byproduct' uses sometimes overshadow the planned uses in value to the company."

As can be seen in Table 2, which lists the various circumstances in which responding executives found it necessary to consult their job

TABLE 2. *Reasons for Most Recent Review or Consultation of Marketing Job Description, on the Basis of 124 Responses*

REASON	NO. OF MENTIONS	PERCENT
Reorganization	23	19
Clarification of responsibilities	22	18
Orientation of new employees	18	15
Performance review	17	14
To update job description (not performance review)	12	10
Review or set objectives	9	7
Recruitment	7	6
Description necessary for new job in department	6	5
To describe contact with other departments	3	2
Salary administration	3	2
Delegation of authority	2	1
At request of personnel department	2	1

descriptions, several reasons for review were predominant. Reorganization of the marketing department, which ranked first, is slightly more prevalent in this respect than the need to clarify responsibilities, which ranked second. One respondent, a manufacturer of household appliances, stated, for example: "We are just redoing job descriptions for our division, as a result of a reorganization; therefore, all descriptions are being examined at this time."

Uses of the Job Description

THE JOB DESCRIPTION usually performs a multiple function. For example, it can serve as a basis for salary administration and at the same time provide a basis for recruitment. The 11 most common uses of the job description in marketing management, in order of prevalence of use by participating companies, are listed in Table 3.

Clarification of Job Responsibilities

Clarification of job responsibilities is the major purpose served by the job description. Seventy-two percent (80 of 111 companies) cite this as the marketing job description's primary purpose. Twenty-eight other participants believe that it is the principal factor to consider when evaluating a job description. One respondent (from an oil refinery) stated: "A good job description should define the relative level of responsibility and accountability within the organization structure and also present an understandable listing of job duties in sufficient detail to properly define the activities."

The spokesman for a large steel company expressed this opinion: "A good [job description] will clearly define, in whatever detail is necessary, by function (categorically), the extent and limitation of responsibility and authority, the basic objectives of the position. . . ." A pharmaceutical manufacturer looks upon this function of the job description as a delineation of responsibilities for the jobholder and his superior: ". . . to define the job for the man and his superior; describe the job requirements in terms of accountability and of know-how or problem solving required of it."

Once the description has been approved, it can serve the cause of corporate harmony in settling conflicts over responsibility and/or authority. One such use was reported by an aircraft manufacturer:

TABLE 3. *Purposes Job Descriptions Serve in Marketing Management, as Reported by 111 Companies* *

PURPOSE	No. of Mentions	Percent
To clarify responsibilities or relationships between jobs	80	72
To set the basis for performance appraisal	51	46
To define or limit authority	39	35
To obtain data for job classification for salary administration	36	32
To clarify job responsibilities for the benefit of other company divisions or departments	35	32
To provide a basis for setting objectives	25	23
To provide a basis for setting standards of performance	24	22
To orient new executives to their jobs	16	14
To set a basis for revision of organization structure	6	5
To assist in executive recruitment	2	2
To identify management development needs	2	2

*Participants were asked to check three items.

"A situation arose in which several functional executives believed they had the authority and responsibility for operations in a particular area. Job descriptions were consulted to determine the appropriate assignment of responsibility and to establish the intent for the assignment."

When the marketing organization outgrows its present organization structure, a manufacturer of farm supplies has found that job descriptions serve still another purpose: "As our volume increases and new jobs are created, the descriptions are consulted for reappraisal and realignment of responsibilities."

PERFORMANCE MEASUREMENT

Recent studies have shown that, as executives have become more committed to managing by results, the job description has increasingly been developed to aid the measurement of individual performance against standards and objectives.

Forty-six percent of the survey participants (51 of 111 companies) state that in recent years greater emphasis has been placed on the use of the job description as a measure of performance and as a

EXHIBIT 1. *A Segment of Position Description and Performance Standards (Rockwell Manufacturing Company)*

JOB IDENTIFICATION NUMBER

TITLE: Director of Advertising	DIVISION:		DATE:
NAME:	DEPARTMENT: Corporate		SECTION:
PREPARED BY:	APPROVED BY: Advertising		

LIST HERE MAJOR SEGMENTS OF POSITION (WHAT INDIVIDUAL HAS TO DO)	WT. %	CLASS 1 2 3	LIST HERE OPPOSITE EACH SEGMENT THE STANDARDS OF PERFORMANCE (CONDITIONS THAT WILL EXIST WHEN EACH SEGMENT IS PERFORMED SATISFACTORILY)
5. Line responsibility for preparing and operating within the limits of the Power Tool Division, International Division, Canadian (except Power Tool) and Corporate advertising budgets.	15	X	5a. When these budgets are submitted for approval on schedule and when they are adhered to throughout the year.
6. Staff responsibility for the preparation of and adherence to the advertising budgets of all other divisions.	5	X	6a. When budgets are submitted on schedule and when ample warning is given to divisions that tend to exceed budgeted expenditures or do not spend according to their budgets.
7. Responsible for corporate identification and transition.	5	X	7a. When promotion and product identification comply with company policies. b. When transition programs are established and on schedule.
8. Responsible for writing and distributing 11 President's Letters and four Management Newsletters each year.	10	X	8a. When letters are written to the satisfaction of the president and distributed on schedule.

means of coordinating corporate objectives with individual goals. Representative statements include the following:

> We have recently initiated a formal program of goal setting to improve performance. Thus the job description has taken on increased importance. [A computer manufacturer]

> The purpose has not changed, but the emphasis has. A job description is now considered an invaluable tool in management evaluation, training, and development. [A glass manufacturer]

> To describe a job in terms of essentials and objectives rather than in terms of day-to-day details and to incorporate measurements of performance. . . . [An electrical-products manufacturer]

> Originally used primarily to define responsibilities. Now used extensively in setting objectives and appraising performance. [An equipment manufacturer]

Rockwell Manufacturing Company has integrated job descriptions with standards of performance. (See Exhibit 1.) The Rockwell job description outlines the function to be performed, the approximate amount of time that should be spent performing the activity, and "conditions that will exist when each segment of the job is performed satisfactorily." While a few of the survey sample job descriptions list performance standards in the body of the description, this particular method of placing the standard side by side with the activity to be performed is not yet common.

Outlines of marketing jobs have tended to become more exact, more definite—primarily to minimize overlap and friction, not to stifle creativity and motivation. The scope of the job is larger; it is no longer an isolated, individual task to be accomplished removed from the mainstream of corporate planning, but is an integral part of a continuing process. In fact, the language of the description may change. One writer sees a new relationship of jobs and activities:

> The organization chart of the future will not describe lines of authority and responsibility in the classic manner, but instead will resemble a systems flow chart that shows the relationship of people and activities to certain defined and specific goals.[1]

---

[1]Charles L. Hughes, *Goal Setting: Key to Individual and Organizational Effectiveness*, American Management Association, New York, 1965, p. 93.

To Define or Limit Authority

An auxiliary use of the job description, often as an amendment to the clarification of the job, is its function of defining or limiting authority.

In 35 percent of the responding companies' statements (39 of 111 companies) this function appears to be coupled with the responsibility factor; for example: "to define relationships, scope of authority, and responsibilities" . . . "to state and clarify their responsibilities and limits of authority" . . . "to identify areas of authority and responsibility."

Salary Administration

The acquisition of data for salary administration was highlighted as a primary purpose of the job description in 32 percent of the companies (36 of 111). This figure is considerably lower than that given in the two previous studies by the American Management Association on the function of the job description, C. L. Bennet's *Defining the Manager's Job* (1958) and Gordon H. Evans' *Managerial Job Descriptions in Manufacturing* (1964). In the former, Bennet mentions that the job description's use for salary administration purposes was very often the first step taken by a company to initiate a job description program. In that study, the salary administration function received 77 percent of the responses (83 of 108 companies). Bennet found that the "description appropriate to salary administration is most often terse and inclined to be specific . . . but the management guide or position guide is inclined to be broad, to stress relationships, and to provide a blueprint for management."

As a result, Bennet stated, "In at least a few companies . . . these programs started with a simple effort to evaluate positions for compensation purposes. Often managers and executives were included in a companywide job evaluation effort. Subsequently, the descriptions were found to be useful in many subsidiary ways—recruiting, orientation, and so forth. Finally, descriptions became an adjunct to organization clarification and planning."

In the Evans study of manufacturing job descriptions, salary administration again received a high number of mentions (nearly 74 percent, or 135 of 183 companies). However, the study points out that:

. . . it is apparent . . . that the staff personnel man or the line manager embarking on a job description program in manufacturing will
want to keep in mind that the descriptions probably will not be used
exclusively for compensation purposes . . . job description programs
are presently aimed at objectives other than salary administration,
but the first "as is" description of a given position is still used for
setting compensation rates.

By the time the survey for the present study was taken in the
summer of 1966, salary administration had become an adjunct to the
primary use of clarifying job responsibilities.

A paper-products manufacturer expressed this change of emphasis: "Originally, [job descriptions] were written for salary administration purposes. Now they are written to outline responsibilities to be
sure [the responsibilities] are all allocated companywide with a minimum of overlap."

To Provide a Basis for Setting Objectives and Standards of Performance

Data from several participating organizations indicate that setting
objectives and determining performance standards through the job
description program are two, closely related elements of the same
management process. This process, or program, of results-oriented
management makes it necessary, usually, to establish objectives and
standards for a manager's position in order that the executive may
be realistically and objectively appraised.

Twenty-three percent (25 of the 111 responding executives) believe
that the job description is important in setting objectives, and twenty-
two percent (24) find it important in setting performance standards.

An oil company, for example, uses the description "to get ideas for
goal setting; to see if any responsibilities are being overlooked."

James L. Hayes, a principal lecturer at AMA's Management
Course, emphasizes the use of the job description as a critical factor
in establishing performance standards, which he believes are important as a basis for management development:

The position description is the best statement of responsibilities
available to us. Often it can be used as an outline of the standards. . . . The position description presumes that the job, as now con-
stituted, is clearly determined. It also presumes that, as the job

changes, the position description will change. I think it is legitimate to say that we cannot develop performance standards (how well responsibilities should be carried out as expressed by the conditions which prevail when the job is done) until good job descriptions are first developed.[2]

Orientation of New Executives

Fourteen percent of the total response (16 of 111 companies) state that one of the most important purposes of job descriptions is to orient new executives to their jobs. For example, the description is used "to discuss the new job with [the incumbent] and assist him in mapping out his job." As reported by a control systems manufacturer: "A month ago a new position was created, reporting to the Vice President of Sales. The incumbent wrote his position description and reviewed and revised the descriptions of those reporting to him."

When new responsibilities were added to a job in a paper-products firm, the description served the same purpose. As a spokesman for the firm stated: "Executive changes required consulting the descriptions to get new men functioning in their new responsibilities, for which job descriptions had been written."

According to a manufacturer of machine tools, the need for reorientation was produced by a reorganization and. reclassification of executive salary structures: "A realignment of responsibilities within the Machine Tool Division has resulted in the rewriting and updating of several job descriptions. This has resulted in the re-evaluation of the jobs' worth with subsequent communications of job changes to the incumbents."

To Set the Basis for Revision of Organization Structure

Only 5 percent (6 companies of 111) report that one of the primary purposes of job descriptions is to set the basis for revision of organization structure. As reported earlier in this study, however, 23 executives indicated reorganization as the reason prompting the most recent review of their job descriptions.

---

[2]James L. Hayes, "Reviewing and Improving the Performance of Managers," American Management Association, New York, 1965, p. 18. An address presented at AMA's Management Course; distributed to Course participants only.

Among the company statements is the following by a systems manufacturer, showing how reorganization affects the use of the job description: "Changing organization required review—reassignment of management level personnel and revision of certain authorities and responsibilities."

A spokesman for an oil company reported: "There have been several recent changes in organization in both the retail sales and wholesale class divisions, and the job descriptions in the changed areas were reviewed. The last instance occurred two weeks ago in retail sales."

To Assist in Executive Recruitment

Although only two companies consider assistance in recruiting executives a primary purpose of the job description, many more note the job description's usefulness in a recent hiring or selection situation. The following statements show how it is used as a guide in recruitment:

> . . . the job description is consulted prior to hiring a brand manager for new products in order to delineate his duties vis-à-vis those of other marketing people already in the company.

> Used to define and describe job for candidates for job openings to aid in gaining a clearcut understanding of what job really is. [A lighting-equipment manufacturer]

> . . . in connection with reorganization of certain areas of responsibility and selection of management people to staff jobs created. [A communications-equipment manufacturer]

The Identification of Management Development Needs

The identification of management development needs as a basic purpose of the job description also elicited very little response. Only two companies referred to this use as primary. It appears, then, that there are other management tools more useful than the job description in assessing management development needs. It may be pointed out, however, that the performance appraisal process, which produces primary information about management development needs, is closely tied to the description of job responsibilities.

The Marketing Concept
and Its Application

THE MARKETING CONCEPT coordinates the many functions of the marketing department and those of other organizational units by channeling them toward a common objective—the customer. In its simplest form, the marketing concept is a marketing program that begins and ends with the customer.

This view is expressed by Ferdinand F. Mauser in *Modern Marketing Management:*

> The rationale of the marketing concept implies that company management makes all decisions in terms of a marketing orientation which begins with the customer. The concept recognizes that the dictator of market success or failure, the customer, is of key concern in determining company policies and actions. All other activities of the business are integrated and balanced in terms of what is best for the company in the marketplace.[3]

Theodore Levitt has expressed the same viewpoint: "Marketing is where the customer is, and it is the customer who in the end decides the fate of the business."[4]

Such a program requires the complete coordination of *all* facets of the marketing activity. Channels must be set up and properly staffed to insure an efficient and profitable organization. If these activities are to be coordinated, the duties of each member of the group must be spelled out, limits of authority established, and reporting relationships outlined.

More important, these duties must be related to each other and to the company. One writer on the principles of marketing has written that before the advent of the marketing concept:

> The sales manager's responsibilities were centered around the management of the sales force; he usually had little voice in product planning, pricing, advertising, and other market planning activities. Advertising was frequently placed in charge of a separate executive with status equal to that of the sales manager. Product planning was

[3]Ferdinand F. Mauser, *Modern Marketing Management*, McGraw-Hill Book Co., Inc., New York, 1961, p. 8.
[4]Theodore Levitt, *Innovation in Marketing*, McGraw-Hill Book Co., Inc., New York, 1962, p. 13.

usually left in the hands of production or engineering executives. In general, the responsibility for performing the various marketing activities was widely dispersed throughout the organization, and often little coordination existed between them. With the advent of difficult competitive conditions, however, business administrators began to realize that the success of the organization depended mainly on how well its products were marketed; they began to see the problem of administering marketing in a different light. They realized that one executive should be placed in charge of all marketing activities, including product planning, pricing, promotion, and selection of distribution channels. Many of the nation's largest firms now have a vice president of marketing whose duty is to supervise all marketing activities.[5]

The preceding statement is reinforced by many of the descriptions submitted for this study; for instance, the Foote Mineral Company's job description position summary for vice president–marketing authorizes the incumbent to "direct and administer marketing functions of the company, including pricing, coordination, distribution, forecasting, customer service, market research and marketing studies, advertising, and public relations." Smith, Kline & French Laboratories places emphasis, in addition, on the responsibility of its vice president, marketing division, to "develop and maintain satisfactory liaison and communications with other Divisions and subsidiaries, with particular emphasis on the Research and Development and Manufacturing Divisions, and with the Marketing Divisions of subsidiaries."

Emphasis on each of the marketing functions has also changed. For example, before this concept was developed, the primary sales job was *to sell*. Now, as Martin Zober has written:

> Salesmen are invited to expand their horizons beyond quotas and the number of calls per customer and to assist others in achieving the long-range, clearly defined objectives of the company. . . . The marketing concept stresses the interaction and interrelationship of selling with the other phases of marketing.[6]

One survey respondent, the Allegheny Ludlum Steel Corporation, uses the job description to define relationships. The corporation's director of sales administration "refers to [job descriptions] regularly

[5]Richard H. Buskirk, *Principles of Marketing: The Management View*, Holt, Rinehart and Winston, Inc., New York, 1966, pp. 9–10.

[6]Martin Zober, *Marketing Management*, John Wiley & Sons, Inc., New York, 1964, p. 147.

in analyzing intradivisional relationships, in conducting manpower audits, and in determining proper classifications of positions."

Also, with advanced technology, selling can now focus on the "needs of the buyer and cover all of them, including the services that may be required to enhance the utility of the product."[7]

To Clarify Job Responsibility for the Benefit of Other Company Divisions or Departments

Nearly one-third of the participants (32 percent, or 35 of 111 companies) believe that the most significant purpose of the job description is to clarify jobs for the benefit of other company divisions. In an effort to eliminate duplication of duties among personnel, many companies make it a practice to outline interdepartmental relationships in detail; typical of their responses are the following:

[The job description] indicates the major functional areas or other specific positions with which position must have primary and continuing working relationship to accomplish position responsibilities, and a brief résumé of the reason such relationship is necessary or essential. [An equipment manufacturer]

. . . clarify relationships and responsibilities between marketing executive positions and other functional executives. [An aircraft manufacturer]

. . . clarify job responsibilities and relationships with operating divisions and other corporate staff entities. [A paper-products manufacturer]

To minimize duplication—encourage harmony between departments. [A refractories company]

. . . to classify working relationships and responsibilities with other departments and to serve as standards against which performance can be measured. [An electrical-products manufacturer]

When the participating companies were asked to indicate whether the character and frequency of marketing contacts with executives of other departments are spelled out in their marketing job descriptions, the percentage of response was much higher.

Relationships with corporate departments are spelled out in 53

---

[7] *Ibid.*, p. 148.

percent of the firms (59 of 111 companies). (See Table 4.) Contacts between marketing and other functions are described 53 percent more frequently in job descriptions of top marketing executives than in job descriptions of subordinates. As the table shows:

- When a job description spells out the character and frequency of contact with executives of other departments, the most frequently described contact is between top marketing management and finance executives (53 percent—31 of 59 companies).

- Nearly half the group (49 percent—29 of 59 companies) state that they describe contact between R&D and their top marketing management, between production and top management, between R&D and market research, and between product service and engineering.

- The R&D and production functions are the most frequently described objects of contact for marketing managers, with engineering following; personnel/marketing contacts are the least frequently described.

- In 44 percent (26 of 59 companies), job descriptions spell out contact between the sales and production functions, between product service and production, and between top marketing management and personnel.

- In 51 percent (30 of 59 companies), contact between the product planning function and R&D is spelled out.

- The least amount of contact described (15 percent—9 of 59 companies) is between the personnel function and the functions of market research, product planning, and product service and also between product service and the finance function.

An example of how the sales function is being enlarged and brought into contact with nonsales activities is the Wyandotte Chemicals Corporation's job description for the director of sales in the industrial chemicals group. The basic function of his job holds him "responsible, in accordance with established corporate and divisional policies, practices, and procedures, for aggressively promoting the sales of Industrial Chemicals Division products through the field sales offices. Responsible for the administrative service necessary in the Operating Divisions Office." However, *in addition*, this executive "supervises technical serv-

TABLE 4. *Degree to Which Character and Frequency of Contacts Between Marketing Functions and Other Corporate Divisions Are Spelled Out in Marketing Job Descriptions, in 59 Companies*

FUNCTION	FINANCE		ENGINEERING		PRODUCTION		R&D		PERSONNEL		INTERNATIONAL SUBSIDIARY	
	No.	Percent	No.	Percent	No.	Percent	No.	Percent	No.	Percent	No.	Percent
Advertising	20	34	15	25	16	27	21	36	14	24	17	29
Market research	15	25	18	31	18	31	29	49	9	15	16	27
Product planning	16	27	24	41	23	39	30	51	9	15	13	22
Sales	21	36	20	34	26	44	18	31	19	32	14	24
Product service	9	15	29	49	26	44	17	29	9	15	11	19
Top management	31	53	27	46	29	49	29	49	26	44	23	39

ice functions. [He is] responsible for the formulation and execution of appropriate advertising policies, plans, and programs in support of sales efforts."

EMPHASIS ON R&D

Another interesting development observed is the extent to which job descriptions of different marketing functions—market research, product planning, and top management—describe contact with research and development. The constant demand for new products, especially in the consumer industries, has emphasized R&D's role.

The Quaker Oats Company's job description for its director, product development, emphasizes this need for the constant flow of new products:

> The incumbent evaluates proposed Grocery Products R&D projects to advise on which projects should be authorized and given what priority. Some of the important criteria considered in establishing project priority are: the project's relation to current and proposed work; its chance of success, from both an R&D and a marketing standpoint; its potential for both long- and short-range profit contribution. Once projects are approved, the incumbent coordinates and expedites development efforts of the various activities involved. The incumbent's involvement continues until the product is marketed nationally.[8]

Several companies detail both intra- and interdivision relationships. For instance, in the W. A. Sheaffer Pen Company the vice president of marketing is instructed to:

> Confer with and collaborate with the President, developing and recommending marketing policies and programs. He confers with and collaborates with heads of other divisional functions, such as Product Research and Development, Manufacturing, Finance, and International, to provide and receive necessary information and to mutually resolve problems involved in the coordination of activities for the achievement of established marketing goals and programs.

Univis, Inc. presented one of the most detailed guides describing "working relationships" submitted for the study; it enumerates 29

---

[8]The complete job description of Quaker Oats Company's director, product development, appears in Appendix B, p. 212.

items illustrating the act or function to be performed and the person whom the incumbent must consult for the effective accomplishment of his duties. Some of the items included are the following:

[The executive] provides to the Vice President for Engineering and Research the market, trade, and special order information necessary for the development and improvement of product design and performance specifications.

Submits to the Vice President for Engineering and Research customer or trade complaints regarding product appearance, specifications, or performance and receives from him reports covering the nature, causes, and extent of customers' returns.

Cooperates with the Manufacturing Division heads regarding the merchandising of products to maintain an even flow of production and maximum utilization of capacity.

Provides to the Vice President for Distribution annual and monthly planned sales figures in product detail in order to furnish the basis for manufacturing releases and for the placement of purchase orders for products purchased for resale.

In the pricing of both regular product lines and new or changed products, counsels with the Executive Vice President and Treasurer in determining the prices to be recommended to the President. This includes informing the Executive Vice President and Treasurer and/or the President in advance of quotation of special prices, terms, or conditions of sales to customer.

Reviews with the Customer Accounts Manager collection procedures currently being followed in an effort to best utilize Marketing Division cooperation and customer acceptance.

Collaborates with the Vice President for Industrial Relations in developing and administering appropriate training programs for supervisors and employees in the Marketing Division.

An innovative approach to outlining relationships between line departments is presented by one oil company. This organization distributes an organization guide to its various regions, providing organization charts, position descriptions, and an activities and relationship chart. Although the job descriptions are some of the briefest submitted for this study, the organization charts, and especially the activities and relationships chart, are quite detailed. A portion of the activities and relationships chart is shown in Exhibit 2. It must be

(Text continues on page 40.)

EXHIBIT 2. PRINCIPAL ACTIVITIES AND RELATIONSHIPS—MARKETING REGION (An Oil Company)

ACTIVITY	APPROVE	ADMINISTER	SUPERVISE	ACT	ADVISE—ASSIST	
					DISTRICT	REGION
A. Service Station Acquisition—Lease/Purchase						
1. Planning and analysis	Marketing Manager	Marketing Manager	District Manager	Real Estate Representative	District Sales Supervisor Dealer/General Representative (Direct) Jobber Representative (Jobber)	Real Estate and Development Manager—Economics and Planning Manager
2. Site selection	Marketing Manager	District Manager	District Manager	Real Estate Representative	District Sales Supervisor Dealer/General Representative (Direct) Jobber Representative (Jobber)	Real Estate and Development Manager
3. Solicitation, negotiation, and justification	— —	District Manager	District Manager	Real Estate Representative	(Jobber) —	Real Estate and Development Manager
4. Acquire zoning variances, use permits, insurance and clear title, etc.	— —	Real Estate and Development Manager District Manager	District Manager	Real Estate Representative	District Engineer	Engineering Manager
5. Acquire building and curb cut permits, utility, services, etc.	— —	District Manager	District Manager	District Engineer	Real Estate Representative	Real Estate and Development Manager Engineering Manager
6. Site layout	District Manager	District Manager	District Manager	District Engineer	District Sales Supervisor Real Estate Representative Dealer/General Representative (Direct) Jobber Representative (Jobber)	Retail Manager —Real Estate and Development Manager— Engineering Manager
7. Construction and equipment estimates	Engineering Manager	District Manager	District Manager	District Engineer	(Jobber) —	Engineering Manager— Purchasing Manager
8. Sales-volume and rent-income estimates	District Manager	District Manager	District Manager District Sales Supervisor	Dealer/General Representative (Direct) Jobber Representative (Jobber)	Real Estate Representative	Retail Manager —Real Estate and Development Manager

EXHIBIT 2 (Cont'd). PRINCIPAL ACTIVITIES AND RELATIONSHIPS—MARKETING REGION (An Oil Company)

ACTIVITY	APPROVE	ADMINISTER	SUPERVISE	ACT	ADVISE—ASSIST	
					DISTRICT	REGION
9. The company's commitment (Proposal-Lease Execution-closing)	Marketing Manager	Real Estate and Development Manager	District Manager	Real Estate Representative	District Manager	Retail Manager
10. Construction and equipment installation	Engineering Manager	Engineering Manager	District Manager	District Engineer	—	—
11. Disposition of documents and related forms	—	—	—	Real Estate and Development Manager	—	—
B. *Service Station Operation—Direct*						
1. Dealer selection	District Manager	District Manager	District Sales Supervisor	Dealer/General Representative	—	Retail Manager
2. Primary dealer training	—	Retail Manager	Retail Training Manager	Retail Instructor	District Manager	—
3. Dealer installation a. Terms and conditions	District Manager	District Manager	District Sales Supervisor	Dealer/General Representative	—	Retail Manager
b. Credit and financial assistance	Credit Manager	District Manager	District Sales Supervisor	Dealer/General Representative	—	Retail Manager
c. The company's Commitment	District Manager	District Manager	District Sales Supervisor	Dealer/General Representative	—	Retail Manager
4. Product sales; merchandising, advertising, sales promotion, and retail programs; and in-station training assistance	—	District Manager	District Sales Supervisor	Dealer/General Representative	—	Retail Manager
5. Customer complaints	District Manager	District Manager	District Sales Supervisor	Dealer/General Representative	—	Retail Manager
6. Business guidance	—	District Manager	District Sales Supervisor	Dealer/General Representative	—	Retail Manager—Credit Manager
7. Collections	—	District Manager	District Sales Supervisor	Dealer/General Representative	—	Credit Manager
8. Lessor relations	—	District Manager	District Manager	Real Estate Representative Jobber Representative (Jobber)	District Sales Supervisor Dealer/General Representative District Engineer	Real Estate and Deveopment Manalger

EXHIBIT 2 (*Concluded*). PRINCIPAL ACTIVITIES AND RELATIONSHIPS—MARKETING REGION (*An Oil Company*)

ACTIVITY	APPROVE	ADMINISTER	SUPERVISE	ACT	ADVISE—ASSIST	
					DISTRICT	REGION
C. Product Pricing						
1. Service stations (salary)—retail prices and services	Marketing Manager	District Manager	District Sales Supervisor	Dealer/General Representative	—	Retail Manager
2. Service station dealers						
a. Automotive gasolines	Marketing Manager	District Manager	District Sales Supervisor	Dealer/General Representative	—	Retail Manager
b. Diesel fuels	Marketing Manager	District Manager	District Sales Supervisor	Dealer/General Representative	—	Fuel Oil Manager
c. Lubricants	Marketing Manager	District Manager	District Sales Supervisor	Dealer/General Representative	—	Industrial/Commercial Manager
d. Specialties and antifreeze	Marketing Manager	District Manager	District Sales Supervisor	Dealer/General Representative	—	Retail Manager
3. Jobbers and tank truck dealers						
a. Automotive gasolines	Marketing Manager	District Manager	District Manager	Jobber Representative	—	Retail Manager
b. Fuel oils	Marketing Manager	District Manager	District Manager	Jobber Representative	—	Fuel Oil Manager
c. Industrial products	Marketing Manager	District Manager	District Manager	Jobber Representative	—	Industrial/-Commercial Manager
d. Specialties and antifreeze	Marketing Manager	District Manager	District Manager	Jobber Representative	—	Retail Manager
4. Industrial/commercial jobbers, tank truck dealers, and consumers						
a. Automotive gasolines	Industrial/Commercial Manager	Industrial/Commercial Manager	Area Industrial/Commercial Manager	Industrial/Commercial Representative	—	Marketing Manager
b. Diesel fuels	Industrial/Commercial Manager	Industrial/Commercial Manager	Area Industrial/Commercial Manager	Industrial/Commercial Representative	—	Fuel Oil Manager
c. Heating oils	Industrial/Commercial Fuel Oil Manager	Industrial/Commercial Manager	Area Industrial/Commercial Manager	Industrial/Commercial Representative	—	Fuel Oil Manager
d. Industrial products	Industrial/Commercial Manager	Industrial/Commercial Manager	Area Industrial/Commercial Manager	Industrial/Commercial Representative	—	—
e. Specialties and antifreeze	Industrial/Commercial Manager	Industrial/Commercial Manager	Area Industrial/Commercial Manager	Industrial/Commercial Representative	—	Retail Manager

remembered, however, that this chart shows a regional breakdown and the duties described are applicable to only one industry.

Following is the complete text of an explanatory memorandum that accompanies the chart:

Marketing's organization has been structured to provide the highest degree of specialization consistent with reasonable span of management control. The organization charts and position descriptions provided in the preceding sections of this guide evidence this approach to specialization. Many activities, however, require participation of multiple units of the organization. In such situations, management personnel are expected to contribute, and should be requested to contribute, to the handling of matters within their provinces.

To illustrate this condition, we have provided a chart of principal activities and relationships in the Marketing Regions. The "line" functions of approval, administration, supervision, and action are specified as being distinct from the "staff" functions of providing advice and assistance.

It is understood that the approval function is limited by the degree of authority delegation. Where a transaction or activity requires a higher level of authority than has been delegated, the matter must be processed through appropriate management levels to the position having adequate authority before final approval can be secured.

Further, the following chart assigns responsibilities to heads of units in the region organization. Many activities, however, will be processed by their assigned staffs without requiring personal participation of the head of the department/activity.

3. Writing the Job Description

THE JOB DESCRIPTION is the most widely accepted method of stating the functions and duties required of a given position. How, then, is the material assembled? What guidelines are there for preparing it?

Job Description Technique

IN JULY 1952 Harold Smiddy, then vice president, management consultation services, and Byron Case, then consultant, management consultation services, of the General Electric Company, wrote an article entitled "Why Write a Description of Your Position?" which was published in the *GE Review*. They described the job description program that was conducted at that time by the General Electric Company, listing the various steps needed to prepare the description and briefly outlining what should be included in each section. The following excerpt from the article indicates the necessary contents of an adequate description:

*Function.** This section summarizes the general functions of the position by stating briefly and succinctly its basic objectives and responsibilities. . . .

Responsibilities and Authority. [This section] lists the major specific responsibilities assigned to the position. Minor responsibilities and duties which are of a routine nature are usually briefed or covered by general language applicable to many positions. The major responsibilities will constitute the objectives of the position referenced to factors or other standards against which performance can be measured and appraised.

---

*Italics in this excerpt have been supplied by the editor.

41

As a general principle, the position should be given authority, to be used with good judgment and as the incumbent sees fit, to do everything that is necessary to accomplish the responsibilities, and hence the objectives, of the position. Authority should be withheld only as warranted and the specific limitations adequately covered by reference to policies and instructions; and where so limited or withheld, the responsibility has to be tailored accordingly. Scope of authority defines an important relationship between the incumbent and his superior; and the superior is the only person who can withhold delegation of authority from the incumbent, realizing that when he does so he inevitably also retains personal responsibility in the undelegated area.

Relationships. This section describes the major relationships that are vital or frequent, both up and down within the line of authority and at all levels outside of the line of authority. The subordinate positions directly supervised by the position being described are usually included.

The fundamental reason for spelling out relationships, either on an Organization Chart or in a Position Description, is to facilitate dynamic organization. The purpose of such organizational tools is to foster understanding of goals, policies, and objectives by all employees, thus creating the most favorable climate so that constructive initiative and voluntary teamwork may be united to give synchronized flow and progress to the work of all individuals jointly and collectively. . . .

Accountability. After objectives have been made clear and the responsibilities and authority defined, the incumbent is accountable to his superior for success or failure in accomplishing these objectives.

The accountability section of the position description records the standards to be used for the measurement of performance. Performance can then be measured and appraised with respect to standards established by objectives and policies as expressed in budgets, scheduled projects, and long-range planning.

The essence of Accountability is threefold. First, executives or supervisors must realize that delegation of authority must be sincere and definite so that they then can fairly hold those to whom it is delegated responsible. Second, responsibility commensurate with such authority must be genuinely accepted and exercised, especially as to decision making, by those to whom it is delegated. Third, accountability then necessarily includes need for personnel policies based on measured performance, defined and enforced standards, and removal for incapacity or poor performance.

The West Penn Power Company has also provided written objectives for its management job descriptions, as is demonstrated in the following excerpt from the company's organization manual:

Position descriptions for top levels of management are developed to:

1. Document plan or organization for management to know and follow.
2. Delegate responsibility and authority in an effective manner in accordance with company's organization objectives.
3. Establish, define, and amend position responsibilities.
4. Maintain effective lines of communication and working relationships.
5. Provide new appointees with details of position.
6. Provide a guide for appraising and rating individual performance and progress.
7. Provide a basis for managerial position evaluation.

Other methods used in structuring job description format are illustrated in Exhibits 3, 4, 5, and 6, which show diverse but effective ways of outlining job duties.

(*Text continues on page 54.*)

Exhibit 3(A). *Example of Job Description Format Structure (International Business Machines Corporation)*

POSITION TITLE_____ PREPARED BY_____
DIVISION_____ LOCATION_____
DEPARTMENT OFFICE_____ DATE_____
REPORTS TO (Name and Title)_____

READ INSTRUCTIONS CAREFULLY BEFORE PROCEEDING

Part I. Description of Position

Purpose of Position: In a sentence or two, what is the primary purpose of your position?

Principal Duties: What are the most important duties you regularly perform? Explain each duty in terms of the end result it is intended to accomplish.

Special Duties: What special duties, task-force assignments, or occasional duties of significance did you perform in the past year?

Exhibit 3(A) *Continued*

PART II. ANALYSIS OF POSITION

In the following sections, analyze your work from three viewpoints: (a) scope of your duties and their impact on Company success; (b) knowledge and skills required to perform your duties; (c) complexity of your duties. Make all statements brief and leave blank any sections inapplicable to your position.

A. SCOPE AND IMPACT

1. *Human Resources:* What positions report directly to you?   None ☐

POSITION TITLE	POSITIONS MANAGED DIRECTLY	
	NUMBER OF EMPLOYEES IN POSITION	NUMBER OF EMPLOYEES MANAGED BY POSITION AT LEFT

Subtotal_____ Subtotal_____ Total_____

In what ways, if any, do your duties influence the selection, placement, counseling, appraisal, and compensation of employees other than those listed above?   None ☐

2. *Market Resources:* In what ways and to what extent does your work directly affect the production of present or future revenue? Specify dollar values where significant.   None ☐

3. *Physical and Financial Resources:* In what ways does your work involve the expenditure, safeguarding, or control of the Company's physical or financial assets (funds, inventory, plant, equipment, costs, vital records)? Specify dollar values where significant.

4. *Other:* In what other ways, if any, beyond those described in (1), (2), and (3) above, does your work affect the short- or long-term business results of the Company?   None ☐

B. KNOWLEDGE AND SKILLS REQUIRED

1. *Specialized Knowledge:* What specialized knowledge is repuired to perform the duties indicated on page 1?

44

Exhibit 3(A) *Concluded*

2. *Other Knowledge or Skill:* What other skills (for example, ability to sell, negotiate, persuade, plan, organize, administer) are required in addition to the specialized knowledge mentioned above?   None ☐

C. COMPLEXITY—CREATIVITY

1. *Planning, Problem Solving, Analysis, Creative Activity:* What are some examples of the planning and problem solving you do that require the greatest degree of ingenuity, resourcefulness, analysis, or creativity?

2. *Decision Making:* What are the most difficult and important final decisions you are called upon to make in the performance of your duties? Indicate whether you share these decisions or whether there are any specific limitations on your decision-making authority.

PART III. ADDITIONAL INFORMATION

Performance Criteria: What performance measurement yardsticks should be used in judging how well the duties listed on page 1 are being performed? Include *quantitative* measures (for example, increase in revenues, cost savings realized, delivery dates met) and *qualitative* measures (such as effectiveness of personnel utilization, accuracy and timeliness of reports, soundness of plans developed).

Additional Comments: Add any other comments regarding your position that help to describe it more fully.

Manager's Comments: I have read this position description carefully and have noted in it all modifications and/or additions I believe appropriate. *(Use space below or extra sheets for additional comments.)*

Reviewed:———————————————— ————————————
                            Manager   Date

EXHIBIT 3(B). *A Segment of an Updated and Slightly Modified Version of Exhibit 3(A) Showing a Method of Illustrating Inside and Outside Marketing Department Relationships of Job Incumbent*

Inside and Outside Relationships: This section is concerned with a position's requirement for exercising judgment and persuasiveness in contacting and dealing with others to secure or exchange information, influence action, and in any other way promote the interest of the IBM Company. (Indicate, by title, personnel with whom you normally have contact, for what purpose, and the frequency with which the contacts occur.)

1. *Inside:* What contacts are required by this position inside the Company?

POSITIONS CONTACTED	PURPOSE	FREQUENCY (DAILY, WEEKLY)

2. *Outside:* What is the extent of contacts with persons outside the Company who are (or potentially could be) engaged in business with IBM or with whom the Company must deal in other matters, such as civic affairs or relations with Government administrative and investigative agencies?

POSITIONS CONTACTED	PURPOSE	FREQUENCY (DAILY, WEEKLY)

46

[Because of changes in organization structure, the following job description, current at the time the survey was taken, is no longer up to date. It is included because of its detailed outline of job responsibilities.]

Purpose: To develop and direct an aggressive and imaginative Marketing program of direct sales, service, and related supporting activities. Determine market opportunities and requirements for existing products, new products, and entirely new fields of market endeavor, to achieve desired share of market and profit objectives.

Authority and Responsibility

Reports to: President

Supervises: Field Sales Managers
Marketing Research and Advertising Manager
Product Manager
Order and Inventory Control Manager

Functional Relationship: Maintains good working relationship with all members of management representing all units of Company. Develops and promotes cooperation between Marketing personnel and all other Company personnel. Develops and maintains good customer relations, public relations, and industry relations.

Authority to Spend Money

Within the limits of the approved budget and up to the following amounts:

Maintenance and Operating Supplies	Replacement of Old Equipment	New Equipment (Change in Operation)
$0,000.00	$0,000.00	$0,000.00

Important Duties and Functions

A. *Planning*
   1. Through personal activities and effective utilization of Marketing management, develops Marketing objectives with short- and long-range Marketing plans and sales strategy to accomplish the objectives.

Exhibit 4 *(Continued)*

2. Through personal activities and Marketing management, plans for the maximum efficiency in utilization of all Marketing resources.

3. Directs the planning for new products to serve market needs, thus assuring greater market penetration and profitability.

4. Reviews and approves recommendations for product-line changes, particularly from the standpoint of profitability, sales volume, sales workload, field selling expense, and trade relations.

5. Directs the development of new markets for the profitable sale of new and future products.

6. Reviews and approves recommendations for Marketing administrative and control policies.

7. Approves distribution policies to be followed by Company outlets and/or distributors and dealers for proper territory coverage.

8. Establishes pricing policy with regard to effect on profitability, sales volume, and customer and trade relations.

9. Directs the development of and approves departmental operational and promotional budgets.

10. Directs the development of and approves sales forecasts and territory sales goals.

11. Counsels and approves the advertising and sales promotion programs required to effectively develop and execute marketing plans and sales strategy.

12. Counsels, approves, and interprets market research program to make policy decisions and recommendations for continued improvement in market position and profitability.

13. Establishes policy for Marketing communications.

14. Establishes policy and approves buying arrangements of products for resale.

15. Directs the development of inventory control plans and activities to assure adequate customer service and an efficient level of inventory turnover.

B. *Organization and Staffing*

1. Develops and recommends the plan of organization required to carry out the responsibilities of the department.

2. Analyzes workforce to maintain adequate level of efficient, trained personnel.

3. Reviews and approves the policies in regard to the recruiting, training, compensation, and evaluation of Marketing personnel.

4. Counsels Field Sales Managers, Marketing Research and Ad-

Exhibit 4 *(Concluded)*

vertising Manager, Product Manager, and Order and Inventory Control Manager in the assignment, promotion, transfer, or dismissal of Marketing management personnel under their supervision.

C. *Direct Sales*

1. Reviews sales performance of all units and initiates action to strengthen sales position.
2. Reviews all customer service activities and initiates action for improvement within Marketing; works with all other units to improve customer services administered by other units of the Company.
3. Stimulates and builds morale of all levels of Marketing personnel through personal contacts in the field.
4. Participates in sales meetings to inform and inspire sales personnel concerning current Marketing objectives and approaches.
5. Personally contacts key accounts and prospects, as necessary, both to support the field sales force and improve customer relations.

D. *General Administration*

1. Analyzes results achieved, against objectives, to measure variances from planned performance in each phase of comprehensive Marketing program; initiates action as required to improve performance.
2. Directs the appraisal of existing products against competitive lines and approves changes to improve competitive situation.
3. Directs the appraisal of new products for sales potential and marketability and directs technical and marketing development for those products that offer prospects for improving profit and market penetration.
4. Represents Company in industry and associational activities.
5. Administers the wage and salary program for Marketing personnel.
6. Maintains good public relations with civic business leaders.
7. Plans, reviews, and approves expenditures for Marketing physical facilities.
8. Promotes good working relationship between Company and all Marketing personnel and demonstrates Company's interest in employees' well-being, personally, socially, and financially.

EXHIBIT 5. *Example of Job Description Format Structure (Cyanamid of Canada, Limited)*

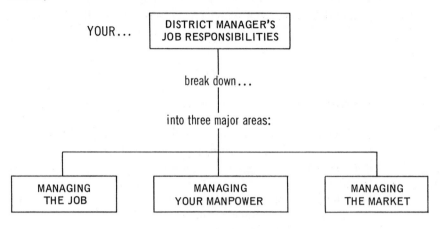

YOUR... DISTRICT MANAGER'S JOB RESPONSIBILITIES

break down...

into three major areas:

| MANAGING THE JOB | MANAGING YOUR MANPOWER | MANAGING THE MARKET |

...so that you can achieve complete DISTRIBUTION of all PRODUCTS and increase their SALES to insure PROFITS for the DISTRICT and CYANAMID OF CANADA, LIMITED.

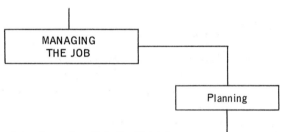

MANAGING THE JOB

Planning

Keep informed of local trends and developments within the District.

Analyze potential and opportunities on which to base recommendations for sales manpower.

Develop the planning and implementation of tactics to attain sales goals and budgets.

  Make sure budget is based on volume it is possible to achieve in the District and territories.

Apply promotions and merchandising programs to the District, and recommend additional promotional activities within the District.

Establish routines for handling recurring decisions.

Organize your time to the best possible advantage.

Develop a schedule of priorities for the job.

Exhibit 5 *(Continued)*

Performance

<u>Measure</u> results against budgets, and take appropriate action to check weaknesses and attain even higher levels of performance.

<u>Insure</u> that provision is made for increasing sales coverage and resulting increased effectiveness of sales representatives.

<u>Check</u> to see whether budget takes into account changes and new developments occurring in District or territories, and inform your Sales Manager.

<u>Maintain</u> an area map of the District.

<u>Make</u> sure financing and credit and credit procedures are followed exactly.

<u>Make</u> periodic calls on customers in company with the sales representative calling on the accounts.

<u>Maintain</u> multilevel contacts with important accounts.

<u>Develop</u> a District analysis to locate weak spots through use of IBM reports.

<u>Report</u> in detail on unsatisfactory conditions with customers, and do what you can to correct them.

<u>Increase</u> sales, and control expenses from the District.

Administration

<u>Submit</u> requests and reports accurately and on time to interested management personnel.

<u>Answer</u> correspondence promptly.

<u>Read</u> all bulletins and other mail.

<u>Keep</u> management informed of developments and changes occurring in the District and territories.

<u>Furnish</u> information required for the preparation of sales forecasts and budgets.

<u>Insure</u> prompt transmission of product-service requests, and follow up.

<u>Inform</u> your Sales Manager of performance against sales forecasts.

EXHIBIT 5 *(Concluded)*

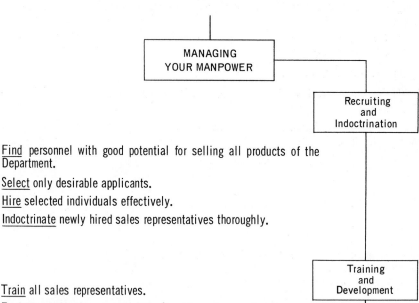

Follow up if orders are not handled on schedule.

Report on product complaints for better production vigilance.

Approve credit authorizations when justified by circumstances, and administer returned-goods policy.

Cooperate with Product Managers and their staffs.

> Self-Development

Analyze your capabilities, limitations, strengths, and weaknesses.

Determine how you can increase your effectiveness.

Establish a schedule for your own development through study and additional training.

> MANAGING
> YOUR MANPOWER

> Recruiting
> and
> Indoctrination

Find personnel with good potential for selling all products of the Department.

Select only desirable applicants.

Hire selected individuals effectively.

Indoctrinate newly hired sales representatives thoroughly.

> Training
> and
> Development

Train all sales representatives.

Evaluate each sales representative's performance regularly.

Plan for each representative's development.

- CONDUCT effective sales and training programs.
- TRAIN men well in each new assignment.
- PROVIDE individual assistance as circumstances dictate.

Exhibit 6. *Example of Job Description Format Structure (American Cyanamid Company)*

```
POSITION TITLE_____ NAME_____
DIVISION_____ REPORTS TO: NAME_____
LOCATION_____            TITLE_____
DEPT. OR SECTION_____ APPROVED BY_____DATE_____
```

1. *Purpose of Position.* Summarize briefly the purpose of your position.

2. Which of your activities do you believe to be most difficult or require the greatest degree of skill? Why?

3. Which of your activities do you believe provides the means for making the greatest contributions to the company? Why?

4. In your present job, describe your own role in seeing that your assigned tasks get done and your assigned functions and responsibilities are carried out (for example, administrator, specialist, teacher, coordinator).

Position Duties

1. *Regular Duties: List and describe below the duties you regularly perform. Give an example or two of the typical problems or projects with which you would normally be concerned. Describe: (a) the problem or project itself (scope, complexity, characteristics) and (b) how you went about planning it and working it out.*

2. *Special or Occasional Duties: List and describe those duties you perform only occasionally or that have been given to you as special assignments.*

Exhibit 6 *(Concluded)*

3. *List commodities, products or product lines, processes, and services with which you are concerned.*

Knowledge, Skills, Experience, and Special Background Required

1. *What knowledge or skills are necessary to carry out your assigned tasks?*

2. *What special skills of negotiating, bargaining, selling, teaching, or persuading others to act are necessary in carrying out your tasks?*

3. *Any other information, knowledge, or experience necessary.*

4. *Summarize the man-specifications you would look for if you were promoted and were asked to recommend your successor.*

Responsibility for Writing the Job Description

THE SURVEY PARTICIPANTS were asked to state who, in marketing management, writes the initial job description. Is it one person, or is the duty shared by several individuals?

Eighty-five percent of the survey participants (94 of 111 companies) responded to these questions. (See Table 5.) In 19 of the 94 responding firms (20 percent), the incumbent has the obligation of writing his own job description. In 17 organizations (18 percent), he shares this responsibility with his immediate superior, and in 18 (19 percent) of the companies the superior alone writes the job description. In 17 other organizations, a company specialist prepares the document.

In only 38 percent of the 94 companies reporting on this question does the job incumbent alone, or the incumbent working with his supervisor, prepare the initial job description. In 7 percent of the participating firms the incumbent works with some other person to do the job. What is fairly remarkable is the high percentage of instances (52 percent) in which the initial job description is prepared by someone other than the incumbent—a company specialist, an immediate superior, a company official, or a consultant. This suggests that participative styles of management have not yet made the extensive inroads in marketing that are often reported.

Most organizations employ the services of company specialists, not to criticize job description content, but to establish uniform standards throughout the organization. In a Midwestern steel company, marketing job descriptions are written by the incumbent, but "to insure some uniformity within the company," the company specialist has the ultimate approval power. At Merck Sharp & Dohme the "first draft [is] generally put together by the immediate superior and the incumbent, then reworked by [the] staff specialist." In IRC, Inc., the description is written by the incumbent but "reviewed by department head, then reviewed with personnel before finalizing." At the Inland Container Corporation the jobholder also writes the initial description, but: "The Personnel Division then rewrites the description in its final form to achieve consistency of format and to check for duplication of job responsibilities. The final draft is approved by the Division Manager and the Personnel Division."

According to the survey findings, outside consultants were rarely called on to write job descriptions. In the few cases mentioned, consultants would usually work with another member of the organization—either the jobholder himself or someone in the personnel department. For instance, during a reorganization period at Allis-Chalmers Manufacturing Company: "Key-position descriptions were

TABLE 5. *Writer of Initial Job Description, in 94 Companies*

INDIVIDUAL(S)	COMPANIES	PERCENT
Incumbent	19	20
Immediate superior	18	19
Incumbent and immediate superior	17	18
Company specialist	17	18
Immediate superior and company specialist	9	10
Incumbent and company specialist	4	4
Incumbent and other company official	3	3
Other company official	3	3
Company specialist and outside consultant	2	2
Incumbent, immediate superior, and other company official	2	2

prepared by members of a company task force who were trained and guided by an outside consultant. . . . The use of company specialists and an outside consultant was a one-time situation for a few key positions."

Other Provisions for Writing the Job Description

IF THE JOBHOLDER does not write his own job description, there are a number of other ways in which information about his job can be obtained. Fifty-six companies (50 percent of 111) provided data on how they do it. (See Table 6.)

In 14 of the 56 companies (25 percent) in which the incumbent does not write his own job description, the person designated to do so receives a good deal of the necessary information about the job during an interview with the incumbent.

In 7 of the 56 companies an interview is coupled with a questionnaire, which the jobholder completes, and observation of work being performed. In eight companies, respondents reported that observation of the duties performed is their sole method of gathering information for preparing a job description—additional evidence that the participative style of management has been resisted in some marketing organizations.

TABLE 6.   *Source of Information for Writer of Job Description, When Other than Jobholder, in 56 Companies*

METHOD	COMPANIES	PERCENT
Interview with jobholder	14	25
Interview with jobholder and observation	9	16
Observation	8	14
Other company official	8	14
Interview with jobholder, questionnaire completed by jobholder, and observation	7	13
Interview with jobholder and consultation with outside company official	5	9
Questionnaire completed by jobholder and observation	3	5
Interview with jobholder and questionnaire completed by jobholder	2	4

Nine of the participants responding to this question mentioned that the jobholder's supervisor is usually consulted, in addition to the other sources of information. For example, C. W. Sanford, of the Crouse Hinds Company, stated: "The supervisor should know what he expects to be accomplished by the jobholder and therefore is best qualified to describe it"; Merck Sharp & Dohme staff personnel drafting job descriptions also conduct interviews with "managers in whose area job falls and those in other areas affected by the job description"; and at Getty Oil Company the supervisors write the job descriptions, "which are then reviewed by the Employee Relations Department prior to being submitted for evaluation."

One company looks to studies conducted by other companies to aid and guide it in clarifying the objectives of its own job description program.

The Future of Job Descriptions in Marketing Management

Do MARKETING EXECUTIVES believe that job descriptions will remain in their present form in their companies for the next five years?

Ninety-four companies replied to this question; 42 believe that marketing job descriptions will remain the same, and 52 cite the need for changes in the form or content of existing descriptions.

Of the 42 executives who believe that job descriptions will remain the same, 35 stated that the descriptions used in their organizations are adequately performing the functions for which they were intended and that therefore they foresee little if any need for change. This view is set forth in the following four statements:

> We basically believe job descriptions will remain in their present form in this large, diversified company, because of their wide use and applicability to outline authority and responsibility. [A large-aircraft manufacturer]

> Existing marketing job descriptions adequately define responsibilities, while flexible enough to cope with changing marketplace. [A home-appliance manufacturer]

> If a job description is complete in outlining relationships, authority, duties, and responsibilities, there would seem to be little that can be added in the foreseeable future. [An electrical-products manufacturer]

> I see no reason for change at this time or in the near future. Job descriptions are needed to clarify responsibility. [An office-supplies manufacturer]

In the fifty-two instances in which change was predicted, twenty-three executives felt that the change would take the form of refinement of the job description; ten see organization changes as having important effects on job descriptions; five see industry changes; three see new job description programs; and one sees "improvement in communication channels" as having a major effect. Some typical comments are the following:

> While minor changes will, no doubt, take place, the functions of the job description in the organization should not change. [An oil company]

> Format will probably remain the same, but content will change. [An electronic-instruments manufacturer]

> We should be able to further improve job descriptions in being usable tools. [A manufacturing organization]

> Corporate growth will require new responsibilities and further fragmentation of authority. If job descriptions are not changed, we will not be able to react quickly. [A cable manufacturer]

> Job descriptions must change as jobs are changed; all jobs change as the nature of the business changes. [A cement manufacturer]

> Changing conditions and changes in emphasis on market require periodic changes in both the marketing organization and marketing positions. [A utility company]

> Jobs and organizations change, and this must be recorded if we are to maintain internal and external relationships. The format will change as required to keep up with new and improved concepts. . . . [A machine-tool manufacturer]

4. Analysis of Job Description Format

Once the writer of the marketing job description has assembled his material, how does he approach the task of organizing it? What items does he include in the job description? How much space does he allot for each item?

This chapter answers these questions and others by examining 587 marketing job descriptions submitted for this study, including those in the Appendixes. These descriptions come from 190 companies participating in the survey and from participants in several AMA Marketing Division programs.

Among the highlights of the topics analyzed are the following:

- Length of the job description.
- Date it was written.
- Title of the document.
- Job title.
- First item to appear in the description and its length.
- Number of items covered in the body of the description.
- Span of control.
- Authority coverage and manner in which it is done.
- Job specifications—percentage of job descriptions that include job specifications.

"Reporting relationships" was among several other items analyzed, but it could not be gauged accurately because it was usually shown by the name of the individual—or names, if there was more than one individual—rather than the function represented.

Length of the Job Description

The length of marketing job descriptions varies from a hundred words (about half a page) to more than eight pages.

TABLE 7. *Length of Marketing Job Description, on the Basis of 587 Sample Descriptions*

No. of Pages	No. of Job Descriptions	Percent
1	112	19
2	247	42
3	125	21
4	62	10
5	21	4
6	11	2
7	4	1
8	5	1

A great many companies, however, prefer one- or two-page job descriptions. Over 61 percent (359) of the 587 job descriptions submitted are of this length, and only 4 percent of the total group (20 job descriptions) are of six pages or longer (Table 7).

The one-page description for the District Sales Manager at the A. O. Smith Corporation (Exhibit 7) is an example of the short, broadly outlined job description used in many of the companies surveyed.

It is interesting to note that four of the five companies that utilize the longest job descriptions received in the survey (eight pages) do so for the function of product manager. One of these companies, B. F. Goodrich, uses such a job description to outline the activities of the product supervisor in the aerospace and defense products division. This document, entitled "Executive Position Information Record," is designed to involve the incumbent totally in writing his own position description, by "providing a framework of reference within which to describe systematically and clearly the content of [his] position and the nature and scope of its functions, duties, responsibilities, and authority, as [he] performs them."

In addition to the customary listing of the person's functions and activities, the format of the B. F. Goodrich job description (Exhibit 8) provides a great deal of space for the incumbent to show chains of command, decision-making procedures, organizational relationships, and so on between himself and his colleagues. If the incumbent does not have all of this information readily available, the process by which he will obtain it will have served in turn to further acquaint him with his co-workers and, more important, to understand the part they play in the performance of his job. As may be seen in Exhibit

8, all sections of this document begin with an introductory and explanatory paragraph, which is followed by a rationale for the particular activity and a listing of applicable activities performed by the jobholder. Perhaps the most detailed listing of job specifications or know-how required of a particular position is shown in this exhibit.

(*Text continues on page 69.*)

EXHIBIT 7. *Management Job Description (Exempt, Corporatewide) A. O. Smith Corporation*

TITLE:	LOCATION:	DIVISION:
District Sales Manager		

WRITTEN BY:	APPROVALS AND DATES:	DEPARTMENT:
POSITION REPORTS TO:	Usually General Sales Manager or Director – Marketing	SECTION:

SUPERVISION EXERCISED:

    0-5   Sales Engineers or Sales Representatives

    0-3   Stenographers

    0-1   Clerk-Order Service

    (plus 0-4 Manufacturers' Agents)

PRIMARY FUNCTION

Directs through subordinate sales representatives or sales engineers and/or manufacturers' agents the phases required to maintain an effective distributive and/or direct sales or contract sales organization in the sale of division's standard, modified, or custom products (annual sales volume approximately $1,000,000 to $3,000,000) in an assigned sales district. Is responsible for the development and coordination of a sales (and/or applications and sales engineering) and service program to secure and maintain a realistic share of the district sales market (through the sale of the most profitable mix of division products) within established cost of sale limits, division and corporate marketing policies. May include negotiation and renegotiation of sales contracts.

The above includes: development of organization, goal setting and follow up to insure that goals are achieved, forecasting, sales programs, market development, customer contact, budgetary cost control, credit investigation, public relations, administration of personnel policies and procedures, and any other duties and responsibilities necessary to achieve departmental objectives.

Division: __Aerospace and Defense Products__ Location:_____ Date:_____

Position Title:__Product/Manager,__   Department Name and Number: Aerospace and Defense Products– Sales–Department 1711

Signed by:_____

Approved by:_____ Director Original Equipment Marketing

_____
Name   Title

General Marketing Manager Aerospace Sales

_____ _____
Name   Title

INTRODUCTION

This *Executive Position Information Record* is to assist you in recording what *you do* in your position. It is intended to provide the framework of reference within which to describe systematically and clearly the content of your position and the nature and scope of its functions, duties, responsibilities, and authority, as you perform them.

From this Position Information Record, it will then be possible to evaluate your position in relation to others in the Company and to establish proper position relationships within and between divisions.

SECTION 1. FUNCTIONAL DESCRIPTION

Briefly, what are the functions of your position?

The major function of this position is to initiate and carry out marketing strategies designed to increase the product-line sales and to maximize the profit position of the assigned group. This function is accomplished by the creation and administration of the product-line business plan that describes the necessary strategies and actions required to maintain an aggressive marketing program. The business plan covers:

    A. Background.
    B. Market potential.
    C. Problems.
    D. Programs.
    E. Strategies.
    F. Cost of the program.

The plan covers all necessary action required by the cognizant Sales, Engineering, and Manufacturing groups. The administrative function of

Exhibit 8 *(Continued)*

coordinating and insuring successful completion of the necessary actions is achieved through directing the Product Management Council as chairman of this group.

SECTION 2. ORGANIZATION CHART

Indicate, by means of an organization chart, the lines of authority existing between your position and your subordinates, your immediate superior, and continuing upward through the organization to the first level of management below the Division President. For Corporate Staff divisions, this will mean the first level below the officer in charge of these divisions. For Research Center, this will mean the first level below the Vice President–Research. Give titles and number of salaried employees under each title reporting to you and below you. Give the number of clock-card or nonsalaried employees under your jurisdiction—that is, reporting immediately to you and at each level below you. Please show separate totals for male and female employees.

General Marketing Manager–Sales
    Director, Original Equipment Marketing
        Product Manager
            Sales Engineer
                Sales Engineer
                    Secretary

The following sections are to guide your thinking as to the kinds of information desired. The statements and questions are to help you in describing your position.

SECTION 3. KNOW-HOW

Know-how is the *sum total* of technical expertise and practical skill, however acquired, required for *acceptable position performance*. It consists of:

1. Practical, specialized, technical, professional, or administrative knowledge.
2. Human skills in motivating, appraising, selecting, organizing, or developing people, singly or collectively.

Know-how has both *breadth* (comprehensiveness) and *depth* (thoroughness). Thus a position may require some knowledge about a lot of things, or a lot of knowledge about a few things. Therefore, describe the know-how required, so that "HOW MUCH KNOWLEDGE ABOUT HOW MANY THINGS" is fully explained.

1. What specialized knowledge, training, and experience do you need?

Exhibit 8 *(Continued)*

2. What length of time is required to obtain the experience, background, and training necessary to fill your position's requirements?
3. How do you apply this knowledge, training, and experience in performing your work?

1. *Knowledge*

   Training and experience to function in this position require a thorough knowledge of fundamental engineering, Company engineering and production capabilities, and customer product requirements. A technical knowledge of rubber manufacturing is essential. Knowledge of market planning, sales management, and business administration is required. The ability to work with customers and immediately analyze any situation that may arise is required.

   To qualify for this position one should have a Bachelor of Science degree in Engineering, with at least two years of product design or other practical technical experience. Additional experience as a Sales Engineer is necessary to understand and make necessary marketing plans and decisions. Knowledge of our products, engineering ability, manufacturing capabilities, scope of the industry, and product usage must be attained through experience in these areas.

2. Length of time required to obtain this experience, background, and training is four–five years of college engineering, three–four years of practical product engineering, two years of sales engineering under close supervision of Product Manager, and two–three years as Sales Engineer without close supervision and with increasing management responsibility.

3. Application of this knowledge, training, and experience consists of preparing product business plans and directing their execution by customer visitation, analysis of customer problems, preparation and presentation of technical and cost proposals, developing sales programs, interpreting and recommending policy, suggesting product developments and improvements, directing the field sales efforts, preparing sales forecasts, setting sales quotas, estimating changes in market trends, directing development efforts in the Engineering Department to products for new or anticipated customer demands, training personnel, and maintaining and expanding the product line.

SECTION 4. PROBLEM SOLVING

Problem solving is the amount of original thinking required by the position for analyzing, evaluating, creating, and reasoning and for arriving at and making conclusions. It has two aspects, or dimensions:
1. The kinds of problems to be solved.
2. The degree of guidance furnished or available in solving problems.

Exhibit 8 *(Continued)*

1. What kinds of problems do you solve under each of the following headings:
    (a) Making the final decisions?
    (b) Defining problems?
    (c) Gathering facts and information?
    (d) Making recommendations?
    (e) Carrying out decisions made by others?
    (f) Scientific experimentation?

2. On what problems do you coordinate the work of others? Work alone? Work for someone else? Work with others?

1. *Kinds of Problems*
    A. Final Decisions
        1. Formulate sales program.
        2. Establish price structure within product lines.
        3. Evaluate potential products.
        4. Determine accounts to be contacted.
        5. Product recommendations to the customer.
        6. Acceptability of contractual requirements and conditions, with help of Legal and Contract Administration departments.
        7. Assignment of duties to personnel.
    B. Defining Problems
        1. Technical requirements to meet customer specifications.
        2. Customer product requirements.
        3. Marketing methods and manpower requirements.
        4. Increase in sales and profits.
        5. Competitive activities for industry as a whole.
        6. Company policy, where higher management or field sales personnel are involved.
        7. Price and quality of our products in relation to competition.
        8. Customer complaints on product performance.
    C. Gathering Facts and Information
        1. Competitive data on prices, service, and performance.
        2. Future product requirements for sales forecasting.
        3. Marketing size and trends.
        4. Future technical or development requirements.
        5. Cost, delivery, and production capacity for establishing quotations.
    D. Making Recommendations
        1. For personnel and facilities to meet quotation requirements.
        2. Marketing methods, prices, and manpower.

65

Exhibit 8 *(Continued)*

        3. Sales policy credit problems.

        4. Sales quota.

        5. Types of advertising material and product brochures.

        6. Company policy on miscellaneous matters.

        7. Marketing plans and programs resulting therefrom.

   E. Carrying out Decisions

        1. Define and execute management policies at the operating level.

        2. Transmit, to field sales organization, decisions on sales policy affecting this product line.

   F. Scientific Experimentation. Limited to recommendations to technical group.

2. A. Coordinate Work of Others

        1. Work of two Sales Engineers and one Secretary.

        2. Sales activity of field organization as pertains to product line.

        3. Activities of factory and staff on problems relative to product line.

   B. Work Alone

        1. Prepare market plans.

        2. Set pricing policy.

        3. Accept orders and contracts.

        4. Supervise activities of assigned personnel.

        5. Prepare sales forecasts and special reports.

        6. Plan and conduct Management Council meetings.

        7. Plan and conduct customer contacts.

        8. Handle customer inquiries, complaints, and special requirements.

        9. Execute actions outlined in business plan.

   C. Work for Someone Else. Specific assignments from higher management, relating to product sales activities.

   D. Work with Others

        1. With other parties concerned with product activity, on problems affecting sales, technical service, cost, production, quality, legal, research, credit, traffic, and purchasing.

        2. With customer purchasing, engineering, or quality control groups, as required.

        3. With field sales organization to further expand product-line sales.

Exhibit 8 *(Continued)*

SECTION 5. ACCOUNTABILITY

Accountability is the measured effect of your position on end results. It has three dimensions, in the following order of importance:

1. The freedom to act. (Standardized, regulated, directed, guided, unguided.)
2. Impact on end results. (Remote, indirect, shared, prime.)
3. Magnitude of the end results that the position most clearly affects.

1. How independent are you from the regulation of others?
2. How do you influence company income or volume?
3. What is the general size of the area(s) most clearly, or primarily, affected by your position? (Wherever possible, report such statistics as total sales, units of production, and number of employees.)

1. *Independence*
   A. Purpose is to accomplish the established sales goal at a maximum profit level. Activities include:
      1. Evaluation of sales potential.
      2. Planning and coordinating sales, technical, and production effort.
      3. Evaluation of product performance versus customer specification.
      4. Increase sales volume.
      5. Establish pricing policies.
      6. Handle customer complaints.
      7. Direct field sales effort.
      8. Supervise assigned personnel.
2. Company income and volume are influenced directly by the activities discussed in Section 1. This is dependent on the accuracy of the market and product plans and the ability to implement these plans.

The Aerospace Accessory product line encompasses seven specified product areas consisting of:
A. Impact Attenuation Systems.
B. Flotation Systems.
C. Aircraft Seat Cushions.
D. Pressure-Sealing Zippers.
E. Thermal Radiation Shields.
F. Space Inflatables.
G. Miscellaneous Aircraft Accessories—consisting of Zippered Panels, Surge Boots, Flexible Connectors, Glare Shields, and Air Duct Seals.

Exhibit 8 *(Concluded)*

Following is a detailed description of the functions involved:

Functions
1. To manage, organize, promote, sell, and service the seven Accessory product areas.
2. Direct product management programs on these products and coordinate all Company activity to promote increased sales and profits.

Activities
1. Coordinate product activities, with responsibility for the improvement of sales, engineering, manufacturing and service of these products.
2. Serve as Chairman of Product Management Council meetings with technical, production, and service departments.
3. Establish pricing policy.
4. Initiate monthly progress reports and special reports for higher management, as required.
5. Supervise activities of two Sales Engineers and one Secretary.
6. Prepare sales and available funds forecasts for higher management.
7. Assist in preparation of sales-promotion material and product brochures.
8. Identify potential customers and product applications.
9. Review and evaluate quotation requests, to determine:
   A. Sales potential.
   B. Compatibility with manufacturing capability.
   C. Profit level attainable.
10. Establish quotations for customer evaluation, including technical proposals and qualification data where applicable.
11. Contact customers, in conjunction with field sales organization, in regard to:
   A. Sales presentation.
   B. Finalization of technical or production programs.
   C. Contract negotiation.
   D. Product difficulties.
   E. Development programs.
12. Provide liaison product information for field sales organization, including price, delivery, contract administration, engineering, and factory service.
13. Issue sales credits, where warranted and approved.
14. Plan and conduct sales conferences with field sales organization.
15. Attend industry symposiums and technical conferences.
16. Evaluate, initiate, and program new products.

DATE

Examination of job description samples shows that 22 percent (127 of 587) were approved six months prior to the survey; 35 percent (203 of 587), two years prior to the survey; 45 descriptions, three years before the survey; 25, four years before the survey; and 40, between 5 and 14 years before the survey was taken. One-fourth of the descriptions (147) were not dated.

An explanation for the absence of a date, perhaps, is the large number of descriptions that have come from company organization manuals. It may be correct to assume, then, that the manuals are updated annually and, therefore, that the descriptions are not dated individually. On the other hand, this may indicate that these job descriptions follow such a rigid format that the jobholder's name and title are fitted into a preprinted page, the content unchanging as the jobholder changes.

Most descriptions that are dated show the date the description becomes effective or the date when final approval is given. It may be found almost anywhere in the description; but, generally, when effective date is shown, it is included in the information box at the beginning of the page showing the jobholder's name, title, location, and so on. When the approval date is given, it is customarily included at the end of the description as a final indication that the

EXHIBIT 9. *Excerpt from Job Description Illustrating a Method of Including Date in Job Description (A. O. Smith Corporation)*

Date	Code
8/20/63	A9820
Supersedes	
Code	Dated
A7820	2/18/63

Title: Director – Economics and Marketing Research		Location: Milwaukee, Wisc.	Division: 01 – General Office
Written by:	Approvals and Dates: 3/21/61	Department: Planning and Marketing	
Position Reports to: Director – Marketing		Section: Economics and Marketing Research	

EXHIBIT 10. *Excerpt from Job Description Illustrating a Method of Including Date in Job Description (A milling company)*

Code: 1-17-30

POSITION DESCRIPTION

Position Title: Director of Advertising	Department: Advertising
Incumbent:	Location: Minneapolis
Reports To: General Sales Manager – Grocery Products	Analyst:
Incumbent's Review: 6-15-60	Date: 12-26-61
Supervisor's Review: 6-15-60	Code:

~~~~~~

---

content listed is an accurate as well as current description of the job.

Exhibit 9 (A. O. Smith Corporation's job description for the director–economics and marketing research) illustrates a different method of including the date in the job description. A milling company's job description for its director of advertising (Exhibit 10) shows the effective date of the document and, in addition, indicates that both the incumbent and his superior have reviewed and agreed on its content.

TITLE OF THE DOCUMENT

The presence in the survey findings of 50 titles for the job description indicates that there is no consensus among marketing management regarding the method of classifying such a document. However, well over half (58 percent) of the 587 job descriptions are headed either by the specific title of the job or by the title "Position Description" or a slight variation of the latter (Table 8). The eight titles shown in the table are at the head of 486 (83 percent) of the descriptions analyzed. In the remaining 101 (17 percent) of the descriptions, a total of 43 additional titles appears. Samples of these are:

- "Position Summary" (9).
- "Position Analysis" (8).
- "Duties of _____" (5).

- "Statement of Functions" (4).
- "Salaried Position Specification" (3).
- "Major Responsibilities and Outline of Duties" (3).
- "Work Activity Guide" (3).
- "Position Description and Analysis" (3).
- "Position Outline" (3).
- "Duties, Responsibilities, and Authority" (2).

The job descriptions that do not begin with the incumbent's job title incorporate it in the body of the job description, usually as a subheading, as in the following example:

Central Soya Co., Inc.

Position Analysis	Merchandising Manager Feed Sales Department
8–25–65	Fort Wayne, Indiana

TABLE 8.   *Title of Job Description, as Shown by 587 Job Descriptions*

TITLE	NO. OF DESCRIPTIONS	PERCENT
Specific title of job; for example, "Vice President, Marketing," or "Director of Marketing Research"	188	32
"Position Description" (Including variations: "Management Position Description" (23), "Exempt Position Description" (20), and "Salaried Position Description" (9)	155	26
"Job Description" (Including variations: "Management Job Description" (7) and "Salaried Job Description" (4)	66	11
"Position Guide"	29	5
"Position Title"	14	2
"Organization Manual"	14	2
"Management Guide"	10	2
"Position Description and Performance Standards"	10	2
Other (See text)	101	17

Job Title

Does the individual's job title accurately define the job being done, or is it a generalized group of words that fits neatly into an organization chart? To find the answer to this question, two other questions were considered:

1. Are job titles consistent by field?
2. Do titles differ greatly by industry?

The survey research found that job titles are generally consistent in a broad field, such as marketing or sales, but vary in the specialized areas, such as marketing research or advertising. For example, the title "Director of Marketing" is used in 13 of the 33 job descriptions examined for this purpose. The second choice in this category is the similar "Marketing Manager," which appeared in ten job descriptions. In some companies, however, a marketing manager is often created for each product. In seven samples, this title appeared as "Director of Marketing [name of] Product."

In the advertising function, however, a greater variety of titles appears because advertising is often combined with sales promotion or public relations. In all, 58 job descriptions were examined; the following list illustrates the preferences found in the job description titles of the heads of the advertising function:

Job Title	Number of Mentions
Advertising Manager	17
Manager–Advertising and Promotion	9
Manager–Advertising and Sales Promotion	6
Sales Promotion Manager	5
Advertising Director	4
Others, receiving one or two mentions each, including Director–Advertising and Public Relations; Coordinator–Advertising and Sales Promotion; and Director–Advertising and Sales	12

Job description format and job titles are fairly consistent among industries. Most marketing departments have a director or vice president of marketing, a director or vice president of sales, or a regional sales staff. Companies with a diversified product line may have several product managers; a director or manager of market research and his staff of analysts; a director of advertising, sales promotion, and/or public relations; and a staff of marketing administrators at the home office. New titles, such as director of marketing planning, appear also.

First Item of the Job Description

Nearly all the job descriptions examined contain some form of job summary statement at the beginning of the description (98 percent, or 574 of 587 descriptions). However, there are variations in length and content.

Ninety-five descriptions label this statement "Basic Function." This total represents 17 percent of the group with summaries; the bulk of the remaining descriptions use modifications of nine other titles. A complete listing is given in Table 9.

The length of this summary statement varies from fewer than 10 words to more than 200. Over half the companies that use summaries (298, or 52 percent) favor short statements of 20 to 50 words. Corning Glass Works' description of the duties of its general sales manager, for example, presents a short, concise statement containing the essence of the duty to be performed:

Purpose of Position:

To plan, direct, and coordinate the sales activities of the division so as to achieve budgeted sales, including budgeted new product sales, while providing for the growth and development of operating margin, personnel, and company penetration in the [name of] market.

Number of Items Listed

The number of items in a marketing job description ranges from 1 to 45 in the companies that participated in the survey. There is the rare company that will give a one-sentence description of a job, and at the other extreme is the company that will show every possible duty of a jobholder to be sure that nothing is omitted.

Most firms, however, take the middle course and list between 8 and 15 items. A full breakdown is given in Table 10.

To see if a similarity exists between marketing executives' duties in different functions, a comparison was drawn by examining 91 job descriptions of the vice president of marketing (24), the marketing

(Text continues on page 76.)

Table 9.   *Title of Summary Statement, as Shown in 574 Marketing Job Descriptions*

Title of Statement	No. of Mentions	Percent
"Basic Function"	95	17
(Including variations, such as "Function," "Primary Function," "General Function," "Chief Function," "Function and Responsibility," "Function and Description," "Primary Function and Responsibility," "Major Function")	136	24
"List of Duties"	57	10
(Including "Principal Duties," "General Statement of Duties")		
"Statement of Job"	20	3
(Including variations, such as "Summary Statement," "Position Summary," "General Statement," "Occupation Summary," "Job Summary")	33	6
"Objectives"	34	6
(Including variations, such as "Accountability Objective," "Job Objective," "Objectives and Responsibilities")	19	3
"Responsibilities"	18	3
(Including variations, such as "Basic Responsibilities," "General Responsibilities," "Duties and Responsibilities," "Primary Responsibilities")	34	6
"Purpose"	40	7
(Including variations, such as "Basic Purpose," "Purpose and Scope," "Purpose of Position")	7	1
"Scope"	10	2
(Including variations, such as "Broad Scope," "Nature and Scope," "General Scope," "Broad Scope of Activity")	8	1
"Organization Relationships"	25	4
"Supervises"	15	3
"Nature of Work"	9	2
(Including "Nature of Activity," "Assignment," "Character of Job")		
Other	14	2

TABLE 10. *Number of Items Listed in a Marketing Job Description, on the Basis of 587 Job Descriptions*

No. of Items		No. of Descriptions	Percent
1 to 7 Items			
1		5	
2		1	
3		3	
4		8	
5		9	
6		22	
7		20	
	Subtotal	68	12
8 to 15 Items			
8		31	
9		38	
10		46	
11		47	
12		36	
13		29	
14		48	
15		36	
	Subtotal	311	53
16 to 25 Items			
16		15	
17		24	
18		19	
19		15	
20		11	
21		13	
22		18	
23		26	
24		8	
25		14	
	Subtotal	163	28
26 to 45 Items			
26		8	
27		7	
28		2	
29		4	
30		1	
31 to 45		23	
	Subtotal	45	8

research manager (45), and the regional sales manager (22). These three functions were chosen because each area represents a marketing activity not closely related to the others. On each job description the first three responsibilities listed were noted, and the predominance compared.

In general, the first duty listed for the vice president of marketing is to direct the sales effort of the company; the second, to formulate marketing policies; and the third, to evaluate new products.

The marketing research manager, on the other hand, is required as his first duty to select and plan market research projects; second, to develop market research objectives, policies, and procedures for his division; third, to conduct market research projects.

The predominant activity in the regional sales manager's job de-

---

Exhibit 11. *Example of Job Description Illustrating Manner in Which Limits of Authority Are Covered (A cosmetics manufacturer)*

ADVERTISING MANAGER

Limits of Authority

1. *On Operations.* Subject to approved budget and schedules, the incumbent has full authority to direct subordinate personnel and advertising agencies in the implementation of advertising programs and to call upon other Company units for such information as may be necessary for this purpose. He is expected to reject or modify advertising and media schedules submitted by the Product Advertising Managers or by the advertising agencies when such schedules do not meet the standards of the Company, and he is also expected to recommend modification of previously approved schedules and programs as may be appropriate. The authority to finally approve advertising schedules, budgets, and allocations, however, is reserved to the Director of Advertising and the Vice President of Advertising.
2. *On Expenditures.* Recommends advertising budgets and allocations and authorizes advertising expenditures when covered by budget. Verifies invoices for advertising and for research services.
3. *On Personnel.* Subject to established personnel policies and procedures, approves status changes for nonexempt employees and recommends status changes for exempt employees.
4. *On Organization.* Recommends changes in size of staff and in product assignments to subordinates.

scription is that of directing the sales effort; second, developing sales goals and objectives; third, supervising and training salesmen.

SPAN OF CONTROL

The span of control of the jobholder is shown in 127 job descriptions (22 percent of 587). The remainder do not describe the scope of supervision exercised by the jobholder. The majority of the job descriptions that mention span of control show from four to six subordinates supervised (43 percent, or 54 of 127) as shown in the following tabulation:

Number of Persons Supervised	Number of Descriptions
1	6
2	11
3	9
4	26
5	15
6	13
7	4
8	4
9	8
10	3
—	—
12	1
13	2
14	1
15	4

Twenty job descriptions show a span of control exceeding 15 persons. These, however, apparently refer to the entire department supervised, not to the number of people reporting directly to the manager.

The span of supervision described usually includes an assistant or assistant manager, a secretary, and a professional staff. Span-of-control figures are given either at the beginning of the job description, in the area where the jobholder's name and title appear, or in an appendix.

AUTHORITY COVERAGE

Limits of authority are seldom outlined in marketing job descriptions; only about a fourth of the job descriptions (24 percent—143 of

587) contain any mention of restrictions on or limits to authority.

In job descriptions where authority is discussed, it is generally described without showing any chain of command or other relationships. For example, Exhibit 11 shows the extent to which authority for the advertising manager of a company that manufactures cosmetics is described. The writer of this job description has clearly outlined limits of authority by subdividing it into four sections: "Operations," "Expenditures," "Personnel," and "Organization."

Where present, the limits of authority section is usually placed at the end of the job description, before performance standards or job specifications, if any.

JOB SPECIFICATIONS

Fourteen percent of the job descriptions (80 of 587 descriptions) contain job specifications. Job specifications are different from the actual job description in that they describe "the mental and physical qualifications of a job, such as experience and skill, which are required of a person to fill it."

Job specifications may take the form of a routine listing of college degrees and company experience, or these items may be coupled with the reasons a person with such experience would be suited for the particular job. For instance, the International Milling Company's description for its general sales manager–grocery products contains the following concise job specifications:

Position Specifications
1. *Education.* College degree in business administration or liberal arts required, with course work in marketing, management, finance, statistics, and public speaking desirable. Graduate work in marketing and management desirable.
2. *Experience.* Minimum of 15 years' business experience with at least 10 years' sales and sales management experience, preferably in the grocery products field, if required. Experience in sales staff areas desirable; exposure to company grain, production, and traffic operations helpful.
3. *Other qualifications.* Must be energetic, with good health, and possess strong leadership ability, sound judgment, and effective sales and administrative ability. Good public speaking ability desirable.

The more detailed approach is also found in the job descriptions of Lorillard Corporation, which illustrate the degree of specificity that some companies use to relate job specifications to job performance. An excerpt from Lorillard's job description for the market research director provides one example of this thoroughness:

Basic educational level. College graduate—statistics and market research major.

Job knowledge and experience. Expert knowledge and experience essential in statistics; mathematics; and planning, establishing, and directing research programs. Application of sampling theory, questionnaire design and working, field administration of interviewers, statistical analysis in all forms, report and graph presentation. Thorough knowledge required of company's sales organization, procedures, and activities of all divisions of the company, particularly of manufacturing, distribution, and advertising; also of company's budgeting methods and procedures as they relate to the field of market research. Over ten years' broad experience in market research and analysis.

Physical and mental demand. Appreciable mental application required in the examination, planning, follow-up, and completion of research assignments. Long-term projects, emergency projects, and other aspects of work require continuous intense concentration and study.

APPENDIXES

A HANDBOOK OF MANAGERIAL JOB
DESCRIPTIONS IN MARKETING

Appendix A—Marketing Management Job Descriptions in Two Companies

THIS SECTION CONTAINS job descriptions for the marketing managements of two companies—General Mills, Inc., a consumer-oriented marketing group, and a Midwest electrical equipment manufacturer.

The job description samples from General Mills, Inc. are organized somewhat "horizontally"—that is, they tend to show the relationships among people in different areas of the marketing department rather than outline a hierarchy of management authority.

The set of job descriptions from the electrical equipment manufacturer, on the other hand, is an example of a "vertical" set of position descriptions, which describe the chain of command from the top marketing official to the area managers in the field sales organization; also included are job descriptions for the heads of marketing research and distributor relations and the controller of the division.

The electrical equipment manufacturer's marketing organization contains four product sales managers (all job descriptions are identical, except for a short section covering each product specialty) and four marketing managers. These managers report to the Product Manager, who, in turn, reports to the Vice President of Marketing. The field sales organization, which consists of division, region, and area managers, and the supporting functions, such as the Manager of Marketing Research, Manager of Distributor Relations, and Division Controller, also report to the Vice President of Marketing.

Each of these job descriptions contains a statement of the major functions of the job and of responsibilities and authority, including detailed statements of responsibility for management, finance, control, organization, and marketing. Also included in many of the descriptions are outlines of responsibility for product planning, personnel and industrial relations, and manufacturing and engineering.

One of the unique features of these job descriptions is a section entitled "Relationships to Others," which clearly defines at greater lengths than most job descriptions submitted the contacts the incumbent has with other members of the marketing department, as well as with individuals in manufacturing, accounting, and personnel divisions.

Representing a consumer marketing organization are the eight job descriptions from General Mills, Inc.—four from the Grocery Products Division, three from the Advertising and Marketing Services Division, and one corporate job description for the head of Advertising. Nearly all these descriptions contain a section outlining job accountabilities and an accountability objective, in which the incumbent is given a broad performance standard against which to measure his job performance. The largest section of these descriptions is labeled "Nature and Scope of Position." This section, which is often divided into subcategories, includes a detailed explanation of how the job fits into the sphere of the product-manager concept.

These job descriptions, like those from the equipment manufacturer, explain reporting relationships in great detail, emphasizing, however, suggested channels of inter- and intradepartmental communications, not chains of command.

I.   General Mills, Inc.

DIRECTOR OF MARKETING

Grocery Products Division

Basic Description

DELEGATION*   List of Job Accountabilities

M   1. Develop and recommend a marketing organization structure which can effectively fulfill the objectives assigned to it, permits the clear definition of accountabilities of key jobs, and has the flexibility to move swiftly in reaction to market problems and opportunities.

---

*Show degree to which the superior is involved in achieving each accountability, as follows:

H — Heavy (deeply involved in producing the consequence).
M — Moderate (involved in key aspects which produce the consequence).
L — Light (involved in a review or overall control sense—usually, after the fact).

L   2. Develop and motivate a marketing team which in quality, depth, and creativeness assures excellent current performance and management continuity.

M   3. Within division policy, formulate and get understanding and acceptance of marketing policies which establish clearly the nature and role of marketing within the department and a constructive environment for the stimulation and support of new ways and new products to market.

L   4. Within division objectives, set aggressive and imaginative marketing objectives for share of market and profitability.
         A. Develop challenging yet achievable volume objectives.
         B. Establish the total market potential for each product line and the portion of those potentials which should be captured by General Mills.

L   5. Coordinate and approve marketing plans which assure an effective and cohesive marketing effort to:
         A. Secure and maintain the desired consumer franchise for each product and product line.
         B. Cultivate the cooperation of the trade and other large-scale buyers.
         C. Render the appropriate profit levels, considering the stage of market development for individual products.

L   6. Ensure that broad ideas and actions for new products and new fields of endeavor are generated within his department and collaborate with Research to ensure that they are marketed on schedule.

L   7. Assure that complete market intelligence is received and properly and speedily analyzed so that market opportunities may be capitalized on as they occur and the effects of competitive activity may be minimized.

L   8. Achieve satisfactory profit and volume performance for individual product lines in relation to preset standards and to general and specific trends within the industry and the economy.

L   9. Develop among marketing groups a cost consciousness whereby all marketing expenditures are weighed against the possible benefits the division might derive.

L   10. Ensure the smooth and economical incorporation of new or changed products into the line through proper coordination with appropriate departments.

L   11. Appraise the accomplishments of his Marketing Managers against objectives, assuring the proper shifts in approach and emphasis when needed.

L   12.   Appraise the effectiveness of advertising agencies and GMI staff groups servicing his marketing groups and assure appropriate corrective action when performance falls below acceptable standards.

I. Accountability Objective

Ensure the short- and medium-term growth of Grocery Products sales volume, profit on sales, and share of the markets in which it competes for his assigned product groups.

II. Nature and Scope of Position

Organization

This position reports to the Division General Manager and is responsible for the overall planning and direction of the Division's marketing operations for several major product groups (as defined in the supplement section).

The marketing operations of the Division are divided between two Directors of Marketing, with each having approximately three Marketing Managers and a Merchandising Manager reporting to him.

Marketing Manager—Functions as Section Head in charge of a marketing team of 2-5 Product Managers and a supporting staff of several Assistant Product Managers and/or Marketing Assistants. Each Marketing Manager is assigned a major product line (i.e., Flour, Cereals, Baking Mixes, etc.) and is held accountable for (A) supervising and coordinating the activities of the Product Managers in development and execution of marketing plans and programs for their respective products and (B) providing the short- and long-term forward planning needed to ensure the profitable growth and expansion of his product line.

Merchandising Manager—Supervise the activities of 1-2 Promotion Managers who function as Trade Merchandising and Promotion Specialists and work closely with the Product Managers in the development and execution of trade merchandising and promotion plans to be incorporated into the marketing program of each product.

Product Management Concept

Under this concept, each Product Manager is assigned one or more products for each of which he develops an annual marketing plan. The plan analyzes the current and foreseeable market conditions for the product and recommends short- and long-term marketing objectives to be achieved, including profit and volume for each product as well as consumer advertising and promotional strategy and programs, trade promotion and merchandising plans, and the budgets required to carry out these activities. Beyond this, the plan states the means to be used for measuring progress toward objectives and the schedule of implementation for each facet of the program (media and promotion schedules, merchandising campaigns, market research, timing, etc.).

In producing his plan and in its implementation, the Product Manager provides direction to the advertising agency on the marketing strategy and development of advertising and promotion plans, and works closely with the assigned Promotion Manager on the development of trade promotions and their timing. In addition, he utilizes the staff services of the corporate Advertising Department particularly on media, packaging and market research problems and works closely with the Sales and Operations Departments to ensure proper coordination of manufacturing, distribution and merchandising aspects of his plan.

Marketing plans feed up to the incumbents through the Marketing Manager level where they undergo a screening and coordinating process. In the pre-planning stage the incumbents are chiefly concerned with reaching agreement with Marketing Managers on the product concept: marketing strategy, short- and long-term goals and objectives, budgetary requirements, etc. Once plans are submitted to them by the Marketing Managers, the incumbents review them not only collectively but individually for balance and creativity and to ensure that the marketing judgments that must be necessarily exercised are derived from as broad a base of facts as can readily be assembled.

Once developed, the plans are reviewed and given final approval by the Division General Manager and Administrative Vice President— Consumer Foods as they progress up through the management review levels. When approved, the plans become the operating blueprint around which division sales and manufacturing organizations program their operations and serve as official authorization for execution of the advertising and promotion programs. The Product Manager is then charged with executing the plan, including recognizing the need for and recommending changes to the plan to overcome market problems and competitive action.

Relationships

The incumbents devote their time primarily to the initiation, coordination, and general supervision of the development and execution of aggressive and imaginative marketing policies and programs. They delegate heavy accountability to the Marketing Managers for the development and execution of marketing plans and the achievement of profit and share of market results. The Marketing Manager keeps the Director informed of variations from planned performance, reaches agreement with him on product concept and marketing objectives, and obtains his approval on proposed marketing programs and subsequent modifications involving a change in objectives, profitability or cost of advertising and merchandising programs. In addition, he keeps the Director as well as division management fully informed on trends and economic marketing conditions which will have an effect on the marketing plans of his group.

In turn, the incumbents are expected to keep the General Manager informed of major variations from planned performance (both favorable and unfavorable), reach agreement with him on broad product concepts and marketing objectives, and obtain his approval on proposed marketing programs. They are also expected to counsel with him on important organizational and internal personnel moves.

While the bulk of marketing-sales-manufacturing coordination is done at levels below this, on key matters such as volume objectives, manufacturing capacity or major policies and problems, the incumbents closely coordinate with the Director of Sales and Director of Operations. Beyond this, the incumbents play a major role in the development of pricing policies and strategies for their product groups.

This position, in collaboration with the Vice President—Advertising and Marketing Services, recommends advertising agency and marketing consultant appointments to the Division General Manager, establishes standard procedures for their guidance by the marketing groups, and supervises the appraisal and control of services rendered by the agencies and consultants.

Although the incumbents are not solely responsible for originating new ideas, considerable emphasis is placed on the determination of market opportunities and requirements for existing products, new products and entirely new fields of endeavor. They must develop an organization where ideas thrive, not only from within, but by stimulating others (e.g., sales and advertising agencies) to come up with well-considered ideas. They then work with the General Manager in pushing these ideas through and collaborate closely with the Executive Food Research Committee in assigning research priorities and assuring that product schedules are met.

DIRECTOR OF MARKETING

(Cereals, Pet Foods, Potatoes, and Casseroles Department)

Supplement

Organization

In this department, the Marketing Managers and their Product Managers are delegated primary responsibility for the development, administration, and control of a complete marketing plan for their assigned products, including both consumer and trade promotions and budgets.

The Merchandising Manager and his staff of Promotion Managers analyze merchandising challenges and problems with respect to the movement of our products through trade channels and the development of new promotional ideas and approaches. They are responsible for developing and recommending what is needed to resolve these problems by way of specific merchandising campaigns and programs, display materials, trade activation, and similar trade promotion plans, as well as the trade budgets required to carry out these programs. Beyond this, they assist in administering these programs and budgets to ensure the most effective expenditure of trade dollars.

Product Lines

The incumbent is the Division's chief marketing executive for the following major product groups:

Cereals	*Pet Foods*
Wheaties	Three Little Kittens
Kix	Speak!
Cheerios	Etc.
Trix	
Jets	
Hi Pro	
Frosty O's	
Goodness Pak	*Potatoes, Casseroles, Etc.*
Total	
Cocoa Puffs	Noodles Romanoff
Twinkles	Pasta Casseroles
Wheat Hearts	Rice Casseroles
Hot Bran	Instant Mashed Potatoes
Protein Plus	Au Gratin Potatoes

Bran with Raisin Flakes   Scalloped Potatoes
Country Corn Flakes   Etc.
Etc.

Dimensions

10 Product Managers.
1–2 Promotion Managers.
9–10 Assistant Product Managers/Marketing Assistants.
7–10 Clerical Staff.
Advertising appropriation limit: $_____.

DIRECTOR OF MARKETING
(*Flour and Mixes Department*)

Supplement

Organization

In this department, the Marketing Managers and their Product Managers are delegated primary responsibility for the development, administration, and control of consumer advertising and promotion plans and programs for their assigned products and work closely with the Merchandising Manager in the development, integration, and coordination of trade merchandising and promotion programs for such products.

The Merchandising Manager has been delegated primary responsibility for the administration and control of trade budgets and the development of merchandising programs as required to ensure the most effective trade acceptance of the Flour and Mix categories. He and his staff of Promotion Managers are responsible for analyzing short- and long-term merchandising challenges and problems with respect to the movement of our products through the trade channels and initiating new promotional ideas and approaches as needed. They develop and work closely with the Product Managers concerned to resolve the problems by way of specific merchandising campaigns and programs, display materials, trade activation and similar trade promotional plans.

Product Lines

The incumbent is the Division's chief marketing executive for the following product groups:

Flour	*Mixes*
GMKT	Saff-O-Life
Gold Medal WONDRA	Softasilk
Red Band	Bisquick
OAB	Pie Crust Mixes
La Pina	Pancake Mixes
DSHP	Muffin Mixes
Etc.	BC Layer Cakes
	Pound Cake
	Angel and Chiffon Cakes
	Gingerbread Mix
	Date Bar Mix
	Brownie Mixes
	Boston Cream Pie
	Pudding Cakes
	Frosting Mixes
	Etc.

Dimensions

3 Marketing Managers.
1 Merchandising Manager.
8 Product Managers.
2 Promotion Managers.
7 Assistant Product Managers/Marketing Assistants.
7-10 Clerical Staff.
Advertising appropriation limit: $_____.

DIRECTOR OF SALES

Grocery Products Division

DELEGATION*   List of Job Accountabilities

M   1. Develop and structure a dynamic selling organization to deliver the product volume programmed and produce the division's profit objective.

A. Ensure proper territorial coverage.

*Show degree to which the superior is involved in achieving each accountability as follows:
H — Heavy (deeply involved in producing the consequence).
M — Moderate (involved in key aspects which produce the consequence).
L — Light (involved in a review or overall control sense—usually, after the fact).

L   2. Develop a field sales force which in quality and depth assures excellent current performance and management continuity.

    A. Ensure that salesmen are properly trained in selling techniques and are up to date with product changes and company sales objectives. Work closely with Personnel Sales Training to develop training programs for salesmen and development programs for managers.

    B. Ensure the development of key subordinates. Establish objective measures and appraise their performance, informing them of their strengths and development needs.

    C. Ensure, through close collaboration with Division Personnel, that compensation policies for sales are equitable and will attract and retain capable people and motivate them to accomplish their objectives.

M   3. Within division policy, formulate and get understanding and acceptance of sales policies which establish clearly the nature and role of sales within the division.

M   4. Collaborate with division management and Marketing Managers to ensure, from a sales standpoint, the establishment of realistic sales volume budgets which are challenging yet achievable and commensurate with profit objectives.

L   5. Ensure that marketing management properly considers the needs and business ways of the trade in developing marketing programs on new and established products.

    A. In collaboration with marketing, establish procedures and controls to ensure proper timing for release of new-product introductions and new-product sales meetings and to ensure that planning letters, promotional write-ups, and merchandising materials are developed and distributed to the sales force sufficiently in advance to permit effective planning and coordination with the trade.

L   6. Ensure that the field sales organization obtains the planned volume of sales within budgeted expense.

    A. Ensure accomplishment of individual zone and region volume and expense budgets by giving them clearly defined objectives and ensuring that they are supported by properly coordinated merchandising programs.

L   7. Ensure, through effective two-way communication with field sales force, that management gets timely notice of market problems and opportunities and competitive activity.

    A. Ensure propagation of successful selling ideas.

    B. Establish an efficient system of sales forms and reports.

L   8. Protect the company's legal responsibilities in all trade relations, ensuring that consumer product complaints are promptly followed through for settlement to avoid possibility of consumer or trade irritation and eventual lawsuits.

L   9. Ensure effective control of sales results and see that corrective action takes place *as* and *when* needed to ensure the achievement of volume objectives within established expense-volume ratios.

ACCOUNTABILITY OBJECTIVE

Ensure that the division achieves its volume objectives for all Grocery Products items at programmed profit and ensure the development of trade contacts, sales programs, operating policies and people necessary to do this.

NATURE AND SCOPE OF POSITION

As Director of Sales for the Grocery Products Division, the incumbent reports to the Division General Manager and heads the National Sales Department, one of the three major operating components in Grocery Products.

Sales operations are national in scope, with approximately _____ different products, including cereals, mixes, family flour, casseroles, and similar items, which are sold on a direct basis to all recognized wholesale groceries and chains. Its customers include about _____ large grocery stores (about _____ of the total), which handle over _____ of the business. They include corporate chains, voluntary chains and cooperatives, and large groceries which do their own warehousing.

To cover this market, the sales force is geographically organized into zones, regions, and districts. Reporting directly to the incumbent is a team of four Zone Sales Managers in the field and a headquarters staff of five Sales Assistants and one Sales Analyst in Minneapolis. The Zone Sales Managers in turn have Region Managers reporting to them, who operate out of regional sales offices.

The Region Manager level is regarded as the front line of action in the execution of marketing and sales programs, with the Zone Sales Manager providing the forward planning and overall guidance needed to ensure an effective and balanced sales effort against zone market potential. Each region has a sales complement of District Managers, Account Managers and Salesmen. District Managers are responsible for training, development and supervision of the field sales force, while Account Managers are mainly responsible for the major account volume as professional key account salesmen.

The principal objectives of the sales force are: (1) to achieve the volume budgets required to accomplish profit targets by product category and (2) to achieve and maintain a high level of distribution through the selling of volume orders on fast-moving products as well as turnover orders on slower-moving items. The sales force must cultivate and stimulate the cooperation of their customers to ensure action and impact on our timetable as contrasted to customer convenience. Good shelf position, support for feature ads, displays, promotions and proper pricing are necessary achievements in the effort to stimulate consumer sales.

Relative to selling per se, the incumbent must be concerned with both planning and execution of sales operations. Sales planning includes setting volume and expense objectives and territory and people realignment to meet changing market conditions. To ensure that plans are properly executed and to keep informed on market conditions, he travels extensively in the field, getting across objectives of campaigns and stimulating zone and regional personnel, attending conventions, solving problems and discussing with major customers their problems and certain product and merchandising ideas.

The incumbent is active, from a sales management standpoint, in decisions involving marketing plans for new-product introduction, market tests, pricing, packaging and promotion, to ensure that such plans and programs fit the need and ways of doing business with the trade. He is assisted by his Zone Managers and sales headquarters staff (specializing by product line), who work closely with marketing, particularly on planning, scheduling, and coordinating the release of promotions to the field; on trade advertising; and field problems. They work on scheduling and delivery problems with manufacturing, on sales to overseas commissaries and also review and analyze sales performance and study specific problems, such as the impact of new distribution channels (e.g., discount houses). Besides guiding his subordinates as required in these types of problems, the incumbent, by working closely with all the marketing echelons during the development of a new product or campaign, ensures that they show proper awareness of the demands of the trade. This includes reviewing package shape, size and identification, space for pricing, trade activators, allowances, pricing structure and markups, etc.

Also reporting to the incumbent administratively is the Director of Merchandising, who functions as Merchandising and Promotion Coordinator for the division. His principal responsibilities are to coordinate overall merchandising activities between the marketing and sales functions, acting in an advisory and consulting capacity as a staff member of division management, and to study broad merchandising problems and challenges with respect to the movement of our products through trade channels.

He also works closely with Personnel on recruiting, sales training, promotions, transfers, and salary administration and with the Comptroller's Department on budgeting, expense evaluation and control, and importantly in the area of profit analysis as it affects sales operations. He works with the Legal Department on all phases of trade promotion programs and performance agreements to ensure proper protection of the company's aims and interest.

Relative to the General Manager, he gets approval on important organizational changes, salaries of key personnel and reviews with him current performance as well as future plans. He is expected to call to the attention of the General Manager important operating factors that may be beyond his jurisdiction in order to highlight the subject matter in the best interest of the division's goals.

DIRECTOR OF CORPORATE ADVERTISING

REPORTS TO: Vice President–Consumer Foods and President

ACCOUNTABILITY OBJECTIVE

Provide the Corporation and Marketing management with timely, valid and significant data and services for marketing decisions relative to markets, media, shows, promotions, etc., continually seeking and validating new and improved methodology and extending services to areas in which, at present, there is no scientific base.

PRINCIPAL ACCOUNTABILITIES (for Organization, Policy Planning, Execution, and Review)

1. Establish and maintain an effective and efficient Corporate Advertising Division capable of efficiently undertaking all facets of projects and services assigned to it.
   a. Establish and maintain clear definition of the accountabilities of functions reporting to him.

2. Develop a team of Corporate Advertising Managers and specialists whose quality and depth assure General Mills of a competence second to none in these areas, and management succession.
3. Formulate and get understanding and acceptance of Corporate Advertising policies and programs which establish clear standards for effectiveness, truth and quality.
4. Provide management with significant, valid and timely market data for decision making and control on the size of markets; market standing of products; effectiveness of advertising; competitors; marketing expenditures; etc.
5. Ensure for General Mills the highest possible return on its advertising investment in media and shows as measured by efficiency in reaching selected audience, audience delivered, and other quantitative and qualitative measures.
6. Ensure the continued development and updating of the Betty Crocker image and services to make her unassailable from a marketing standpoint.
7. Provide Marketing with services in the areas of consumer promotions, packaging planning, advertising accounting which keep it at the forefront of developments in these areas.
8. Establish effective contacts with counterparts in industry and in advertising fraternity so as to maintain at the forefront of developments in his field.
9. Accomplish Corporate Advertising results for General Mills that establish and maintain it always equal to, and often ahead of, competitors in know-how and overall marketing effectiveness.

NATURE AND SCOPE OF THE POSITION

The Corporate Advertising Division, headed by the incumbent, provides management with specialized services in the following areas:

Packaging Planning: These are specialists in package design and package production who act as liaison between Marketing and the design agency and the manufacturer. Their chief concerns are with quality of materials and graphics, ease with which a product would be identifiable on a store shelf, typography, functionality, etc.

Media and Shows: The Company uses five advertising agencies which, along with the proposed advertising program, recommend the media and shows to be used. The product profile developed by Marketing establishes the customer for the product and therefore the audience which must be reached. This function must, therefore, evaluate how successful the agencies' proposals would be in reaching this audience, if necessary by subjecting the proposal to pretesting. They must also decide whether spots should be used or the message should be part of the program and how best the requirements for several different products can be brought together for a coherent marketing program.

Consumer Promotions: This is a service function to Grocery Products Marketing, advising it, relative to proposed consumer promotions, on the best method to achieve the desired effect, the cost of doing it, and likely returns that will be derived. This section also administers all the consumer promotions once they are put into effect. To give an idea of the magnitude of these promotions, it should be mentioned that people are employed in the advertising warehouse and in the Coupon Service section where coupons come in annually. Indispensable to this service is the need to screen and evaluate continuously the many premium suggestions coming in from manufacturers and agencies specializing in this field so as to provide product managers with the most novel premiums available. Assistance is also given to groups such as churches, schools and other associations in the development of programs to save coupons to be redeemed on some special piece of equipment—a school bus for example.

Market Research: This section provides market research services mostly to Grocery Products Marketing management for the gathering and analysis of data relative to the size and location of markets and up-to-date data on positions or specific products in that market, both General Mills and competition. The department can substantially aid the effectiveness of marketing through the development of effective means of pretesting products and proposed marketing programs so that consumer reaction can be predicted. This can save the substantial cost of going into a test market with a product. In addition to serving Grocery Products, this department provides market-research-derived services, information and analysis to the three preceding sections and to other divisions.

Betty Crocker Kitchens: The Kitchens serve as a base for the Betty Crocker image, which is a strong link with the consumer. Specifically, they prepare directions on packages and increase the market for products by developing variations of standard recipes and adding new recipes that can be used by Marketing as a theme for selling the product. They also prepare the recipes for cookbooks, maintain recipe records, and prepare food for photographing and TV.

Advertising Services and Betty Crocker Enterprises: The latter half of this title comes from the job of being the business manager and publisher of the *Betty Crocker Cookbook;* the former half relates to photography, print production and art services.

Advertising Accounting: This section checks invoices received from advertising agencies against authorizations and budgets assures that the agency has obtained all the volume discounts to which the Company is entitled, and clears the invoices for payment.

Also reporting to the incumbent are an Advertising and a Merchandising Manager for nongrocery products. In such cases, advertising is done largely in trade publications and merchandising related to providing sales training materials and exhibits at industry shows.

The services of this division and the advertising which it buys are mostly for the Grocery Products Division, which does nearly all of the Company's consumer advertising and promotion. It is, however, responsible for the corporate advertising, and incumbent must keep the desired corporate image in mind in screening advertising programs and selecting media and shows. Because of the amount of money involved, the selection and purchase of media and shows are prime concerns of this job.

Other concerns are to maintain a fresh, up-to-date image of Betty Crocker which can be used effectively by the Company in its marketing program and in guiding Marketing and agencies in its use. Relative to all services, incumbent is continuously concerned that they meet the requirements of the divisions, that there is a continuous effort made to improve the services and carry them into areas where there is a need for them.

Because the division's services are largely for the Grocery Products Division, the incumbent must work closely with Grocery Products Marketing management to ensure that its requirements and needs are being met. He also works closely with advertising agency personnel and is one of the management members who recommend to the President the assignment of agencies to products and also the hiring and firing of agencies. Since he is the Company's purchaser of shows, he also maintains close contacts with the major media and networks so as to be apprised in advance of the vehicles likely to be available. The incumbent is a member of the Association of National Advertisers and the Advertising Federation of America.

DIRECTOR OF MARKETING RESEARCH

Delegation*

    I.   Purpose

        Provide guidance and leadership in directing the Corporation's marketing research efforts to those *critical* problems

---

*Show degree to which the superior is involved in achieving each accountability as follows:
H—Heavy (deeply involved in producing the consequence).
M—Moderate (involved in key aspects which produce the consequence).
L— Light (involved in a review or overall control sense—usually, after the fact).

and decisions to which the development and application
of marketing research promise to yield the greatest opportunities for minimizing risks and maximizing profits and
in administering the Corporation's marketing research expenditures in such a way as to represent the optimum
utilization of these funds.

II. ACCOUNTABILITIES

M
1. Provide the Corporation with guidance and direction
in *identifying* those critical problems and decisions to
which the application of marketing research promises
to yield the greatest opportunities for minimizing risks
and maximizing profits.

L
2. Provide the Corporation with guidance and direction
in developing budgetary programs designed to support
systematically planned programs of forward-looking marketing research and, upon obtaining management
approval of these programs, administer them in such
a way as to ensure the *optimum deployment* of the marketing research manpower and dollar resources made
available by them.

L
3. Ensure that all marketing research administered in
behalf of the Corporation is initiated, implemented,
and interpreted in such a way as to maximize its
actionability and profitability, enabling management to
pursue a course of action on the basis of the research
with the assurance that the reduced risks involved in
following this course of action will result in savings or
additional earnings that will more than offset the
costs of the research.

L
4. Ensure that every marketing research project implemented by or for the Marketing Research Department
in behalf of the Corporation is designed, executed,
and reported in accordance with the highest quality
standards consistent with its probable impact on risk
reduction and profit improvement.

L
5. Guide and direct the Marketing Research Department in the *development and validation* of new and improved market research techniques for measuring and
predicting the reactions of consumers, both adults
and children, to our own and our competition's products, packaging, advertising, merchandising, and other

marketing approaches, thereby enabling the Corporation to increase the competitive advantage that it has attained over its major competitors through the development and application of more sophisticated marketing research.

L   6. Through publications, conferences, and contacts with other marketing research people, ensure that the Marketing Research Department keeps fully informed of all new developments in the field of marketing research technology, evaluating those techniques and services which are conceptually sound and adopting those which measure up to acceptable standards of sensitivity, reliability, and validity, thereby ensuring that all marketing research undertaken in behalf of the Corporation is based upon the consistent application of the most advanced techniques and services available.

L   7. By means of bulletins and presentations, keep all levels of management *apprised* of significant developments in the field of marketing research and of the progress and results of all major marketing research projects undertaken by the Corporation.

L   8. Provide corporate and divisional management with personal *counsel and service* in connection with the initiation, implementation, and interpretation of those marketing research projects having the greatest potential impact on corporate and divisional profits, ensuring that these projects are assigned appropriate priorities and are administered in the most expeditious manner possible.

H   9. Provide corporate, divisional, and marketing management with the counsel and services of a *professionally competent staff* of business-oriented marketing research generalists and specialists, well trained in the disciplines of statistics and the behavioral sciences and experienced in the practice of consumer research and market analysis to ensure that all marketing research undertaken in behalf of the Corporation—whether implemented internally through the staff-service sections of the Marketing Research Department or externally through the facilities of consultants, research agencies, or the research departments of advertising agencies or media—measures up to acceptable standards of sensitivity, reliability, and validity to justify its use as a basis for decision making at each of the various levels of management involved.

L   10.   Ensure that the Corporation is making the most effective use possible of the counsel and services offered by reputable marketing research consultants and agencies and by the research departments of advertising agencies and media, through systematic review and objective appraisal of their facilities.

M   11.   Formulate, establish, and promote understanding of departmental goals and objectives and of the policies and procedures aimed at ensuring their attainment.

H   12.   Develop and maintain an organization structure geared to the evolving marketing research needs of the Corporation, clearly defining all accountabilities so as to ensure the attainment of departmental goals and objectives.

L   13.   Select, develop, and motivate, through effective guidance and leadership and through the practice of sound remuneration principles, a staff of marketing research personnel representing sufficient breadth and depth of professional competence to provide the Corporation with the counsel and service it currently requires and also to ensure continuity of marketing research manpower and marketing research management.

L   14.   Develop and recommend a departmental budgetary program geared to the marketing research needs of the Corporation and control expenses within the limitations of this program as approved (or as subsequently amended), ensuring that these funds are administered in such a way as to represent the most efficient utilization of the marketing research manpower and dollar resources provided by the program.

III. NATURE AND SCOPE

The incumbent reports to the Vice President, Advertising and Marketing Services. His principal working relationships include the heads of the various operating divisions (particularly those within the Consumer Foods Activity) and the various corporate staff departments (particularly Public Relations, Quality Control, Central Research and Corporate Development).

He also establishes and maintains such relationships outside the company with:

Suppliers of continuing subscriber services.

Marketing research agencies offering general and specialized services.

Research departments of GMI's advertising (and package design) agencies.

Governmental agencies; professional, industrial, and trade associations; advertising media; and other sources of marketing information.

The Marketing Research Department primarily services the Grocery Products Division in the same manner as the rest of the Advertising and Marketing Services organization; i.e., a small portion of the service rendered is to the other entities of the corporation.

The primary areas of the incumbent's position are: (1) providing leadership to the corporation concerning the effect that sound marketing research can have on product success; (2) providing effective *applied marketing research* service to the corporation; (3) providing the latest and most *effective marketing research tools* to enhance the success of the corporation; (4) providing expertise in *general administration* of the department to maximize its effectiveness; and (5) providing assistance ensuring the accomplishment of *special projects* of corporate significance effectively and efficiently.

In providing leadership the incumbent gives periodic presentations to key members of management to interpret the function of marketing research as well as to report developmental research activity. News bulletins are also used in this capacity.

Applied marketing research is provided through the departmental organization. The key phases of applied research are: (1) problem identification—isolating the problem and screening it for actionability in terms of reducing risk and maximizing profit; (2) implementation of the study; and (3) interpretation of the study findings to management.

Development of effective marketing research tools is of major importance. New problems may require new tools for effective and efficient solution. Existing techniques command improvement to provide the competitive edge required in today's business world. An optimum balance of effort toward basic research and applied research is required to ensure success in marketing research activity.

In general administration, the incumbent is involved in planning, organizing, staffing, directing and controlling and is highly concerned to ensure that projects are initiated and followed up properly, while maintaining security and complying with clearance procedures.

As a primary concern, the incumbent is personally involved in special projects of concern to corporate management. These special projects may include studies concerning the effectiveness of corporate symbols, images, and/or personalities, as well as other projects as necessary.

The incumbent's department is organized with the following key personnel reporting to him:

Marketing Research Director for Grocery Products. The primary functions of the section headed by the incumbent of this position are the exact isolation and precise definition of marketing problems and the interpretation of findings of project studies undertaken in attempting to solve the marketing problem. Other important phases of the section's work include the approval of project study design, execution, and study results. (Within this section is a planning and new products area that concentrates on the use of ideas, concepts and communication techniques to uncover unfilled product needs and to find the most promising answers to the greatest needs.)

Marketing Research Manager—Corporate and Other Projects. The incumbent of this position services the needs of nongrocery product operations in the same manner as the Marketing Research Director for Grocery Products. He services the corporate staff departments and other divisions in their marketing research needs.

Director of Consumer Research. The section headed by the incumbent is primarily concerned with the implementation phase of those project studies which can be more effectively handled within the company than outside and especially those projects with a high value in terms of the marketing decision concerned and the relative importance of the risk factor therein. Projects that are also handled inside are security cases and projects involving the utilization of special, unique techniques. This section also assists in departmental training, the collection and processing of data, as well as the coordination of various technical services.

Manager of Test Market Research and Special Analyses. The incumbent of this position guides his section in providing support to the Marketing Research Managers of the department. The section's primary focus is on the movement of products from GMI through the wholesale and trade level into the hands of the ultimate consumer. However, this section is also involved in recommending and analyzing test-market and merchandising experiments which are prime concerns. Problems for analysis are received from the Marketing Research Managers after they have been identified and defined. Thus the work involves designing studies, implementing and analyzing them. Interpretation of the study is also made by the section and presented to the Marketing Research Managers.

Staff Economist and Business Analyst. The incumbent's (of this position) activity centers around knowing where to find economic and business data in general and ability to recognize their applications to the food and chemical industry and to General Mills specifically. His main areas of concentration are: analysis of business trends, consumer movement analysis, management presentations, special requests for economic and business analysis, and forecasting.

Staff Psychologist. The incumbent of this position provides guidance and counsel to the department in such areas as psychological characteristics of public images, questionnaire development, group interviews, personnel advice, and the need and effect of adding new services to the department.

Staff Statistician. The incumbent of this position guides his section in providing service to both the department and to the various operating divisions and corporate staff departments—in the consultant capacity and in the actual performance of statistical analyses, as well as in the development of new statistical procedures and techniques.

Marketing Research Librarian. The incumbent of this position maintains collections of research reports, books, periodicals, and other information. Special requests are filled through borrowing from other sources or purchasing. The Librarian's prime function is to provide service to the department through maintaining a well-organized, systematic collection of information.

In conclusion, the Director of the Marketing Research Department provides marketing research leadership to the corporation; provides effective applied marketing research; provides new, effective marketing research tools and techniques to aid competitiveness; provides expertise in general administration to maximize effectiveness; and provides assistance, ensuring that special projects of corporatewide significance are effectively and expeditiously carried out.

DIRECTOR OF PLANNING AND NEW PRODUCTS

I. PURPOSE

To develop feasibility studies for new product development, recommend new products to be developed, and coordinate the development of products approved for development.

II. ACCOUNTABILITIES

1. Develop and structure an effective organization with clearly defined rules capable of successfully meeting all the challenges of the department.
2. Select and motivate a staff which, in quality and depth, assures excellent current performance and management continuity.
3. Develop and recommend to the General Manager the complete four-year divisional product development program, for both existing and new products, which will contribute toward meeting and exceeding the division's profit objective.
4. Ensure that management is advised of new product opportunities, alternative courses for development of new products, and the probable results of such developments.
5. Ensure the development of a program, in conjunction with the Corporate Planning and Development departments, aimed at potential business acquisitions in those product categories which will contribute toward meeting or exceeding the division's profit objectives.
6. Ensure the identification, analysis, reporting, and recommendation of new product categories with growth potential not currently marketed by the Division.
7. Ensure the compilation and development of information which will correctly reflect the progress of a new product's development.
   a. Provide management with the necessary information and recommendations which will facilitate their decision responsibilities of continuing or abandoning a new product's development.
8. Ensure that the Executive Food Research Committee (EFRC) is presented with projects for approval as and when needed.
   a. Ensure continuing appraisal of progress on all new products approved by the EFRC.
9. Ensure that the Canadian operations are fully advised, as and when necessary, of new product development by the U.S. Grocery Products Division and Central Research and provide advice and guidance on the feasibility and desirability of developing new products.

III. RELATIONSHIPS

The incumbent reports to the General Manager of the Grocery Products Division. He has constant contact with Marketing, Central Research Laboratories, Operations, Treasury, Controller, and Distribution. He also has contact with the Executive Food Research Committee.

IV. Scope and General Nature

The Planning and New Products Department is responsible for ensuring that management is advised of new product opportunities, alternative courses for development of new products, and the probable results of a new product's development. It is the Department's responsibility to effectively develop feasibility studies and recommendations for presentation and management approval and to coordinate the development of new products which management has approved.

The incumbent is assisted by and provides direction to the Planning and New Products Manager and the New Product Planning Manager. Reporting to them are four New Product Planners and the Research Production Coordinator.

With the concurrence of the General Manager, the incumbent is responsible for determining which new product categories are to be studied by his Department and for assigning them to the proper Planning and New Products Manager for the development of a feasibility study.

Such a study requires careful development of the different facets of a new product's potential, cost, and problems to be encountered in developing the product and final marketing to the consumer. The study will bring out the alternative ways of proceeding with a new product's development and implementation as a marketable commodity, whether through acquisition, subcontracting, or development of the necessary facilities by GMI. Each alternative plan will embrace the capital investment required, together with the anticipated effect on the Division. The criteria are growth, profits, and return on stockholder's equity.

When the Planning and New Products Department has completed the study and prepared the recommendations, the incumbent will then make the decision on what will be the recommendation to the General Manager and then to the Executive Food Research Committee.

When a new product has been approved by the EFRC, it is a part of the Division's Applied Product Research Program and is assigned to the Central Research Laboratories. A marketing group is assigned to the category by the General Manager. At this point coordination is critical in order to have a smooth transition and transmission of information. The Department must coordinate the preparation, endorsement, approval, and distribution of the Applied Product Development Authorization form, which is the master record of all projects in the applied research program. (The current status is kept of all projects in such program.) It is also the responsibility of the Planning and New Products Department to cooperate and assist the assigned Marketing Department and the Research Development Team in bringing to a successful conclusion the recommendation which has been made by the Department. The Department is responsible for the coordination of the development efforts of the Divisional departments.

As the various developmental phases are completed, pertinent data must be compiled to ensure complete communication with Division and Marketing Management. A report is submitted to the Executive Food Research Committee on the progress of new product developments, including recommendations whether such developments should continue, be canceled, or set aside for consideration at a future date.

The incumbent must assemble, analyze, and develop all pertinent information which will permit the timely accomplishment of the Division's future plans and the basis for sound recommendations to management. Through the development of this material it is possible to correctly reflect the product's progress and the problems being encountered and to base recommendations of continuation or cancellation of development to the EFRC.

The incumbent must develop information on all new products for the two long-range planning sessions each year. It is his responsibility to contact (and get agreement to be programmed) Research, Grocery Products Marketing, Grocery Products Operations, Grocery Products Accounting, and Corporate Engineering. The overall plans are then transferred to Grocery Products management in the new product timing and priority meeting. The Grocery Product Plans are then formally transferred to Research Management via appropriate meetings and written reports.

Certain forms, schedules, and systems are used to facilitate the discharge of these duties. Among these are:

a. The Grocery Products Plans Folder, which includes the Division's current year's:
    1. Capital Requirements Forecast.
    2. New Product Marketing Schedule.
    3. New Product Production Planning Schedule.
    4. Research Write-out Schedule, by Marketing Group.
    5. Executive Food Research Committee Schedule.
    6. New Category Analysis Schedule.

b. The Cereal/Snack Facility Plan, which outlines the long-range timing of major capital outlays.

c. The Applied Product Development Authorizations System, which is the master record of all projects included in the Applied Research Program.

It is from this material that the incumbent is able to keep management advised as to the progress of a project's development, advising as to delays and increased costs and the reasons therefor. From such information and recommendation provided by the incumbent, the Executive Food Research Committee will base its decision to continue or abandon the development of a new product.

The incumbent is secretary of the Executive Food Research Committee. This committee is responsible for approving products for development and during a product's development to approve continuation or abandonment of a product's development. The purpose is to ensure that research time is devoted only to those products which will eventually be marketed and which appear to have strong potential from the outset. As secretary, the incumbent ensures that matters of paramount importance are brought before the EFRC and that the necessary information and recommendations are presented to facilitate the committee's decision responsibilities. In addition, the incumbent will provide the means of disseminating pertinent material to departments necessarily involved in a product's development.

The development of the feasibility studies and the assembly, analysis, and development of information during a product's development necessitate close collaboration with a number of General Mills departments, such as the Central Research Laboratories, Marketing Department, Division and Corporate Engineering, Distribution and Finance. If a new product being considered for development necessitates or involves an "established business" acquisition, the department must work with the Corporate Planning and Corporate Development departments for determination of the desirability and feasibility of acquiring a specific established business. In those instances where Corporate Planning is considering the acquisition of, or has been confronted with an offer of sale by, an established business with products applicable to GMI's Grocery Products Division, Corporate Planning will request a study regarding the economic value and appropriateness of the specific products for GMI and as to Grocery Products Division interest.

Since all information pertaining to a new product and its development is confidential, the incumbent is responsible for maintaining complete security with inhis department and taking what steps are necessary to prevent the information from being "downgraded" outside of his department. It is his responsibility to determine what information should be presented to various information sources while developing feasibility studies which will be sufficient to gather complete and comprehensive information for the study and to provide other departments with only the information necessary for the particular assignment.

The Planning and New Products Department provides a liaison with the Canadian office on new product development. They keep them advised on new product development being carried on by the U.S. Grocery Products Division and Central Research. In addition, they will provide advice and guidance on the feasibility and desirability of developing a new product.

The incumbent is expected to accomplish his objectives with little technical guidance. His primary responsibilities are to assess, on a continuing basis, his organization, people, and objectives in order to develop an organization structure and assign people within that structure in a way that will most effectively accomplish his objectives. He is continually confronted with the problem of developing a staff capable of quickly changing from one project to another; therefore, the incumbent 'must have intimate knowledge of the technical and personal strengths and weaknesses of his people in order to achieve maximum productivity.

DIRECTOR, MEDIA AND SHOWS

DELEGATION*

    I. PURPOSE

        Develop, direct, coordinate, and evaluate all Media and Shows activity, especially the negotiation of all media purchases, consistent with marketing objectives, to effectively and efficiently obtain the greatest value from the expenditure of advertising dollars.

    II. ACCOUNTABILITIES

L   1. Develop and recommend media plans and policies, consistent with long- and short-range marketing ob-

---

*Show degree to which the superior is involved in achieving each accountability as follows:

H — Heavy (deeply involved in producing the consequence).
M — Moderate (involved in key aspects which produce the consequence).
L — Light (involved in a review or overall control sense—usually, after the fact).

jectives, to effectively guide the company in the expenditure of advertising dollars.

L   2. Establish policies, procedures, and performance standards to effectively and efficiently direct the purchase of both print and broadcast media, the production of commercials, and the provision of audiovisual services.

L   3. Develop and maintain an organization structure that will successfully achieve the goals and objectives of the Media and Shows Department.

L   4. Select, develop, and motivate a staff of competent managers and specialists who in quality and in depth will ensure excellent current and future performance and maintain high-level management continuity.

L   5. Ensure the coordination, direction and consolidation of media purchasing requirements to qualify for all advertising discounts available, consistent with sound marketing objectives, and negotiate such purchases in concert with agency representatives.

L   6. Ensure the maintenance of favorable relationships with all broadcast and print media representatives, to obtain optimum media purchases and sustain the company's high-level public image.

L   7. Ensure the thorough evaluation of all Media and Shows activity, including media purchases, to maintain or increase the effectiveness of the Media and Shows Department.

L   8. Establish and maintain standards of quality and types of programming, for the different media, which General Mills considers compatible with its corporate and product image.

L   9. Maintain continuing awareness of broadcast and print media developments and trends, to enable General Mills to make the best possible plans for advertising. Disseminate this information to those who need to know.

III.   NATURE AND SCOPE

The incumbent, who is the head of the Media and Shows Department, reports to the Vice President of Advertising and Marketing Services. While the Media and Shows departmental services have corporatewide application, their nature makes them more closely related to consumer marketing, with the result that 90 percent or more of the work undertaken is directly or indirectly for the Grocery Products Division.

Reporting directly to the incumbent are:

Supervisor, Broadcast Media: The role of the Supervisor, Broadcast Media, is fourfold, and refers to spot television and broadcast media purchasing. It includes the evaluation of purchase recommendations, consolidation of purchases, negotiation of discount structures for purchases, and follow-up or review of purchases.

Recommendations for spot television and broadcast purchases are made by the advertising agencies. The recommendations are evaluated by the incumbent, together with the Manager, Media Research, to determine whether the proposed media purchase(s) will reach the profile of customers desired and realize the anticipated results or not. All purchases are consolidated, when possible, depending on products and agencies, and coordinated to qualify for the greatest discounts. In the negotiation stage, consolidated purchases, discounts, time on local stations or networks, and programs are crystallized. After a purchase plan is approved and completed, it is closely followed and evaluated in terms of whether the media purchased realized the goal of reaching the product's best customer efficiently and effectively.

Manager, Print Media: Print Media includes newspapers, magazines, periodicals, transportation, and outdoor advertising. The incumbent evaluates purchase recommendations from the agency, consolidates purchases desired, negotiates purchases, and reviews the purchases made.

Manager, Media Research: The incumbent is responsible for the gathering, analysis, and reporting of data related to media activities and problems. He does not conduct all media research himself. However, he ensures that all media research is accomplished, as indicated by the continuous increase in assistance provided by the various syndicated services to which GMI subscribes. Media information includes broadcast and print audience characteristics by households, persons, cumulative audiences, reach and frequency, duplication, cost per 1,000, etc. Competitive tracking also is within this information-gathering area. All competitive activity is monitored for scope and effort.

Another important phase of the incumbent's work, along with information gathering and analysis, is the evaluation of agency recommendations for media purchases. This is accomplished in concert with the other members of the Media and Shows Department, as applicable.

Broadcast Production Manager: The incumbent oversees the production of television commercials, ensures that all measures are taken by agency personnel to provide quality production in balance with economical cost in the best interests of the company, and remains available for consultation on any and all phases of commercials production. He also oversees the audiovisual operation within the department.

All commercial production work is awarded after being processed through competitive bidding. All bids, complete with storyboards, and agency recommendations are reviewed prior to the establishment of production schedules. All factors affecting commercial costs are thoroughly checked to effect the greatest savings. Quality control is exercised through review and participation in storyboard approval, preproduction meetings, shootings, rushes, interlocks, and answer prints. Thus, as well as providing consultant service, the incumbent administers the functions of cost control and quality control.

The audiovisual activity encompasses three basic functions: the production of motion pictures and filmstrips, the distribution of motion pictures and filmstrips, and the provision of audiovisual service throughout the general office. Film pictures are produced by the incumbent and outside producers, depending upon costs and facilities available. Complete production arrangements are handled by this section. Distribution, the biggest phase of audiovisual services, includes issue, receipt, inspection, repair, storage, and reissue. Distribution of films and filmstrips averages ___ and ___ per month respectively during the school year.

This section also provides audiovisual service for the general office. Approximately _____ audiovisual requests for service are filled per month. Projection facilities include the auditorium, directors' meeting room, G. P. conference room, and the screening room. The film and commercial library is also maintained by this section.

The Manager, Media and Shows, provides coordination direction to the above section heads of his department. While this is a basic function of his position, he also recommends and establishes overall policies and/or procedures affecting all areas of responsibility within Media and Shows. He also establishes and maintains proper standards of performance for all areas within Media and Shows. He ensures that all recommendations and negotiations for media purchases are efficient and effective in terms of the marketing plans and the objectives of the various corporate divisions.

The incumbent's relationships are many and varied. Within the company he provides background data, counsel, and advice in connection with media purchases to Division General Managers and Directors of Marketing. He also works with the Marketing Managers on advertising plan development and execution.

Contacts outside the company are primarily with television network personnel, radio network personnel, print media personnel, individual station personnel and/or their representatives, and program suppliers.

In summary, the Media and Shows activity has the primary function to give specific as well as broad overall direction to our media purchases, to coordinate the many individual requirements of brands and product groups, to evaluate recommendations of agencies, and to maintain optimum relationships with all the media and show suppliers. In fulfilling this function it is essential not only that Management and Marketing personnel be kept up to date on broad trends and new developments in media but also that the marketing groups keep the Media and Shows Department apprised of their needs and of any contemplated changes in existing programs. The Media and Shows Department also maintains direct contact with the media departments of all agencies in coordination with the marketing groups, as involved.

MARKETING MANAGER

DELEGATION*

M 1. Recommend changes in basic structure and complement of his marketing group as necessary to ensure the effective fulfillment of objectives assigned to it and provide the flexibility to move swiftly in relation to marketing problems and opportunities.

L 2. Develop and stimulate a marketing team which in quality, depth, and technical competence assures excellent current

------

*Show degree to which the superior is involved in achieving each accountability as follows:

H — Heavy (deeply involved in producing the consequence).
M — Moderate (involved in key aspects which produce the consequence).
L — Light (involved in a review or overall control sense—usually, after the fact).

performance and provides qualified successors for key marketing positions within the group.

    A.   Provide a clear definition of accountabilities for all jobs and ensure complete understanding and acceptance of these accountabilities by the individuals concerned.

    B.   Establish performance standards for all key positions, continually evaluate performance against these standards, and take necessary corrective action to prevent substandard results.

M   3.   Within division objectives, ensure that aggressive and imaginative marketing goals are established for share of market and profitability of each product.

    A.   Develop and recommend challenging yet achievable volume objectives.

    B.   Establish the total market potential for each product and recommend the portion of those potentials which should be captured by General Mills.

M   4.   Ensure that sound marketing strategies and plans are developed by the Product Managers which will:

    A.   Secure and maintain the desired consumer franchise for each product.

    B.   Cultivate the cooperation of the trade and other large-scale buyers.

    C.   Render appropriate profit levels, considering the stage of market development for the individual products.

M   5.   Ensure that broad ideas and actions for new products and new fields of endeavor are generated within his marketing group and collaborate closely with Research to ensure that they are marketed on schedule.

L   6.   Assure that complete market intelligence is received and properly and speedily analyzed so that market opportunities may be capitalized on as they occur and the effects of competitive activity may be minimized.

H   7.   Develop and recommend pricing strategy for his group of products, which will result in the greatest possible share of market for each product over the long run.

M   8.   Achieve satisfactory profit/loss ratio and share of market performance in relation to preset standards and to general and specific trends within the industry and the economy.

M   9.   Ensure effective control of marketing results and see that corrective action takes place *as* and *when* needed to ensure the achievement of marketing objectives within approved budgets.

    A. Continually evaluate consumer and trade reaction to advertising programs, merchandising deals, and promotions, as well as product packaging and formulation, and ensure the timely adjustment of marketing strategy and plans to meet changing market and competitive conditions.

    B. Appraise the effectiveness of advertising agencies and GMI staff departments servicing his marketing group and assure appropriate corrective action if performance falls below acceptable standards.

L   10. Recommend changes in divisional marketing philosophy and policy when it is felt that such changes serve the best interests of his marketing group and of the division in the long run.

I. ACCOUNTABILITY OBJECTIVE

Ensure the short- and medium-term growth of Grocery Products sales volume, profit on sales, and share of the markets in which it competes, for his assigned products.

II NATURE AND SCOPE OF POSITION

Organization

The marketing operations of the division are divided between two Directors of Marketing, each having approximately three Marketing Managers and a Merchandising Manager reporting to him.

Marketing Manager: Functions as Section Head in charge of a marketing team of two-five Product Managers and a supporting staff of several Assistant Product Managers and/or Marketing Assistants. Each Marketing Manager is assigned a major product line (i.e., Flour, Cereals, Baking Mixes, etc.) and is held accountable for (a) supervising and coordinating the activities of the Product Managers in the development and execution of marketing plans and programs for their respective products and (b) for providing the short- and long-term forward planning needed to ensure the profitable growth and expansion of his product line.

Merchandising Manager: Supervises the activities of one-two Promotion Managers, who function as Trade Merchandising and Promotion Specialists in the development and execution of trade merchandising and promotion plans to be incorporated into the marketing program of each product.

GMI Product Management Concept

Under this concept, each Product Manager is assigned one or more products, for each of which he develops an annual marketing plan. This plan analyzes the current and foreseeable market conditions for the product and recommends short- and long-term marketing objectives to be achieved, including profit and volume for each product, as well as consumer advertising and promotional strategy and programs, trade promotion and merchandising plans, and the budgets required to carry out these activities. Beyond this, the plan states the means to be used for measuring progress toward objectives and the schedule of implementation for each facet of the program (media and promotion schedules, merchandising campaigns, market research, timing, etc.).

In producing his plan and in its implementation, the Product Manager provides direction to the advertising agency on the marketing strategy and development of advertising and promotion plans and works closely with the assigned Promotion Manager on the development of trade promotions and their timing. In addition, he utilizes, as needed, the staff services of the Corporate Advertising Department, particularly on media, packaging, and market research problems, and works closely with the Sales and Operations Departments to ensure proper coordination of manufacturing, distribution, and merchandising aspects of his marketing plan.

Once developed, the plans are sent up to and approved by the Marketing Manager, Director of Marketing, Division General Manager, and Administrative Vice President—Consumer Foods levels. When approved, the plans become the operating blueprint around which division sales and manufacturing organizations program their operations and serve as official authorization for execution of the advertising and promotion programs. The Product Manager is then charged with executing the plan, including recognizing the need for and recommending changes to the plan to overcome market problems and competitive action.

During the preplanning stage, the Marketing Manager works closely with each of his Product Managers in arriving at basic market strategy and the short- and long-range profit and share of market objectives proposed for each product. Beyond this, each Product Manager is basically responsible for initiating and following through the planning, development, and execution of the marketing plan for his product, the Marketing Manager providing a counseling and coordinating role in the coordination of those elements which cut across product lines and in resolving nonroutine problems and decisions that are beyond the Product Manager's scope of responsibility.

Relationships

The Directors of Marketing devote their time primarily to overall guidance and coordination of the Division's marketing program for their product groups, while delegating heavy accountability to the Marketing Managers for the development and execution of broad as well as specific marketing plans and the achievement of profit and share of market results. The Marketing Managers are expected to keep the Directors informed of variations from plan performance, reach agreement with them on product concept and marketing objectives, and obtain their approval on proposed marketing programs and subsequent modifications involving a change in objectives, profitability, or cost of advertising and merchandising programs. In addition, they are expected to keep the Directors, as well as division management, fully informed on the trends and economic marketing conditions which will have an effect on the marketing plans of their respective groups.

As part of their forward-planning responsibility, the Marketing Managers are expected to prepare periodic long- and short-range industry and product projections relating to their category of products, working in conjunction with Marketing Research, Planning and New Products, Operations, and other divisional departments concerned to recommend facilities, capacity, and product availability.

They are expected to look at the market opportunities and requirements for existing products, new products, and entirely new fields of endeavor and work closely with the Director of Planning and New Products, as well as the Executive Food Research Committee, to ensure that marketing opportunities are followed through and developed.

In addition, they are expected to recommend sound pricing policies for their group of products on the basis of careful analysis of cost/price/ profit ratios.

They seek the advice of headquarters and field sales management on the timing, concept, and programming of trade activation programs; timing and location of test marketing, as well as new product introductions; and proposed price changes.

Their administrative responsibilities include participation in the selection of candidates for marketing positions within their groups; reviewing and evaluating the performance and progress of each member of their team, taking necessary corrective action to prevent substandard results; formulating and conducting training programs to develop, maintain, and stimulate toward innovation an efficient product management group; and participating in the development of operating policies and procedures for their groups for approval by the Directors of Marketing and Division General Manager.

They must ensure that avenues of communication are open between their marketing groups and other operating departments within the division so that information necessary for marketing decisions and mutual understanding of problems will be exchanged. They work closely with other Marketing Managers to stimulate free communication between the different marketing groups so that a cross-fertilization of new marketing ideas and concepts will result. In addition, they provide the necessary support to their product management teams in getting needed resources and securing top-level approval for promising marketing ideas and concepts and in soliciting support from other operating or staff groups that might otherwise not wish to be distracted from interests of their own.

The Marketing Manager provides functional guidance over the activities of a Marketing Research Representative assigned to his group in planning the marketing research studies that are needed to guide the development of marketing plans and coordinates the allocation of expense and priority of these studies for his particular marketing group.

MARKETING MANAGERS
(*Cereals, Pet Foods, Potatoes, and Casseroles Department*)

Supplement

Organization

In this department, the Marketing Managers and their Product Managers are delegated primary responsibility for the development, administration, and control of a complete marketing plan for their assigned products, including both consumer and trade promotions and budgets.

The Merchandising Manager and his staff of Promotion Managers analyze merchandising challenges and problems with respect to the movement of our products through trade channels and the development of new promotional ideas and approaches. They are responsible for developing and recommending what is needed to resolve these problems by way of specific merchandising campaigns and programs, display materials, trade activation, and similar trade promotion plans, as well as the trade budgets required to carry out these programs. Beyond these responsibilities, they administer these programs and budgets to ensure the most effective expenditure of trade dollars.

MARKETING MANAGERS
(*Flour and Mixes Department*)

Supplement

Organization

In this department, the Marketing Managers and their Product Managers are delegated primary responsibility for the development, administration, and control of consumer advertising and promotion plans and programs for their assigned products and work closely with the Merchandising Manager in the development, integration, and coordination of trade merchandising and promotion programs for such products.

The Merchandising Manager has been delegated primary responsibility for the administration and control of trade budgets and the development of merchandising programs, as required, to ensure the most effective trade acceptance of the Flour and Mix categories. He and his staff of Promotion Managers are responsible for analyzing short- and long-term merchandising challenges and problems with respect to the movement of our products through the trade channels and for initiating new promotional ideas and approaches as needed. They work closely with the Product Managers concerned to resolve these problems by way of specific merchandising campaigns and programs, display materials, trade activation, and similar trade promotion plans.

MANAGER OF CREATIVE SERVICES

DELEGATION*

    I. PURPOSE

        Provide the Corporation and all divisions with the latest in high-quality creative services in the areas of packaging, art, photography, and printing production, as well as in related special request areas. Serves as the company consultant for Creative Services.

---

*Show degree to which the superior is involved in achieving each accountability as follows:

H — Heavy (deeply involved in producing the consequence).
M — Moderate (involved in key aspects which produce the consequence).
L — Light (involved in a review or overall control sense—usually, after the fact).

II. Accountabilities

M   1. Recommend and establish plans and objectives, both short- and long-range, to guide the Creative Services organization in providing effective and efficient service to meet and fill the needs of the Grocery Products Division and other company operations.

L   2. Establish and maintain an organization structure, clearly defining all key accountabilities, capable of effective and efficient accomplishment of creative service requests and/or assignments.

L   3. Select and develop a team of managers and specialists who in quality and depth will provide excellent current and future performance, ensuring long-range management continuity.

   a. Ensure that effective art direction is provided, assuring that creative designs, layouts, and concepts produced by our Art Department are capable of communicating the intended message and of optimum artistic and technical quality.

   b. Ensure that all creative service personnel keep abreast of new developments in their respective fields and adopt items applicable to the needs of GMI to sustain it at the forefront of the field.

L   4. Ensure that expenditures are optimized in the creative services field through effective liaison within GMI and between GMI and all outside creative service contacts.

L   5. Ensure that the quality of package work done throughout the Creative Services Department meets appropriate standards with regard to marketing objectives, technical and artistic quality, and corporate needs.

L   6. Ensure the provision of advice and counsel concerning any phase of creative service activity; i.e., packaging, merchandising tools, visual aids, photography, etc.

L   7. Ensure the effective procurement of all printed packaging to meet advertising and merchandising production needs, in balance with economy to obtain the greatest mileage from the funds expended.

L   8. Ensure the effective financial administration of all creative service activities, maintaining and safeguarding all equipment, inventories, and facilities, assuring sound usage of the dollar.

L   9. Ensure the effective control of the movement of all advertising materials through the company, ensuring that all clearances are timely, thereby aiding in keeping advertising costs at a minimum.

L   10. Ensure the effective and efficient accomplishment of all special projects or requests accepted by the Creative Services Department.

L   11. Develop and recommend a departmental budgetary program (including adjustments thereto); and, upon approval, control expenses incurred by that program without sacrificing effectiveness in operations. Initiate studies for cost improvements without negating effectiveness.

M   12. Ensure that all advertising materials meet GMI standards through the development and maintenance of necessary clearance procedures.

L   13. Ensure that relationships are maintained with outside art and design suppliers so that the company has available top-quality creative talent for those efforts which cannot be handled internally.

III. NATURE AND SCOPE

The incumbent reports to the Vice President–Advertising and Marketing Services. He has contact with all staff departments and operating divisions throughout the company although 90 percent of his department's work is in servicing the needs of the Grocery Products Division. In coordinating the package planning function he has close working relationships with Package Research, Manufacturing, Engineering, Quality Control, Purchasing, the various marketing and sales departments, and Accounting. The incumbent is responsible for the administration of the Creative Services complex.

Reporting to the incumbent are the heads of the following functions:

Package Design: Package design is based on sound marketing principles as well as art and design. It is the application of art and design to marketing. A package design must be one that will attract the market profile best suited for a product as established by the Product Manager.

General Mills procures package designs from industrial designers, independent artists and designers, and within the Company. It is the role of the Supervisor, Package Design, to supervise the procurement of package designs, to design packages, to provide art direction, and to act in the capacity of the company's liaison control agent, ensuring that the packaging design needs of the company are properly fulfilled with the ultimate in effectiveness and evaluating fidelity of design and photography to intention.

In that packaging is a dynamic industry, fashionable and yet expanding by leaps and bounds, a major problem is keeping up to date. The fashion problem in packaging is compounded by the activity of competition.

Print Production and Art Services: This functional area is separated into Art Services, which provides services that are almost endless in number, and Print Production, which provides advice and guidance concerning various phases and methods of printing and the procurement of printed needs as requested. In general, the artist services provided are in the following categories: merchandising tools (consumer and trade activation material, recipe books, visual aids, publications) and packaging (for consumer products, including flour and other items as requested). All requests for work are coordinated to ensure effective and efficient accomplishment, whether within or outside the Company. Work that is not within the scope of the section or cannot be worked into the schedule is sent out for full or partial completion, according to the needs of the situation. The print production function is specialized for advice and guidance requirements needed in the purchase of printed advertising and merchandising materials—i.e., trade magazine inserts, advertising reprints, merchandising tools, etc. Each job is a custom job requiring special handling with final evaluation; all factors are considered on an individual job basis without the sacrifice of standards and quality levels.

Photography: A complete photo studio is operated to provide photographic services that are equal to or better than the quality of such services available elsewhere. The ultimate in effective illustrations is created. All types of still photography are done, in black and white and color, for advertisements, cookbooks, package faces, filmstrips, slides, portraits, scientific projects, etc. Factors in performing these services are ability to provide immediate service of top quality and at a substantially lower cost than comparable outside services.

Package Production: This function, related to purchasing as well as others, ensures that all packages are produced to our best advantage, suiting all of our needs. The current usual methods for printing packages are lithography and gravure. The Supervisor, Package Printing, purchases positive litho plates for the lithography method. For gravure, he selects the printer and the gravure cylinder maker even though he does not buy the gravure cylinder. By purchasing the positive plates and selecting the maker of the cylinder, he can attain greater control on the quality of final product. The proofs of both the plates and the cylinders are reviewed for taste appeal, color accuracy, and faithfulness to the transparency, illustration, or keyline.

The Package Production section maintains close liaison with the printers throughout the printing process. A morning and afternoon review of the printing run is made daily concurrent with printing operations to ensure that standards are met and that the desired printing quality is maintained.

Advertising Traffic: Coordination is the byword of this function. The movement of all advertising materials through the company while they are being reviewed for approval requires close coordination to ensure knowledge of whereabouts at all times. Advertising materials are proposed advertisements, in various stages of preparation, for use on radio, television, and in print media. This material is received from the advertising agencies for review and clearance by all people and departments concerned. It must move on schedule and be returned to the agency, meeting all deadlines.

Depending on the content of the advertising, clearance may be required from any or all of the following: Vice President, Advertising and Marketing Services, Betty Crocker Kitchens, Legal Department, Product Manager, and Marketing Manager. After it has been completed and has been cleared by all, the advertising material is returned to the agency.

This section maintains slide files and a library of all GMI print advertising and television commercials respectively, keeps all interested parties informed of GMI TV and radio programs and print schedules, monitors programs for accuracy and clarity, ensuring that commercials are correctly scheduled and presented on the proper shows on the proper dates.

While the Manager, Creative Services, is in charge of overall management of Creative Services, he also personally administers many special projects that may be of divisional, corporate, or industrywide significance; e.g., division signature, corporate symbol, and/or a governmental inquiry into the food industry and its packaging techniques. Even though the special projects are time consuming, the incumbent's primary emphasis is on package planning and the overall Creative Service complex.

II. A Manufacturer of Electrical Products

VICE PRESIDENT–MARKETING

I. FUNCTIONS

The Vice President–Marketing is the chief executive of the Marketing Division and, as such, is responsible for the efficient operation of the Division and for achieving the maximum volume of profitable sales throughout the Company.

He is responsible for carrying out all policies and procedures established by the President and the Board of Directors.

II. RESPONSIBILITIES AND AUTHORITY

Within the limits of his approved program and Company policies and control procedures, the Vice President–Marketing is responsible for, and has commensurate authority to accomplish, the fulfillment of the duties set forth below. He may delegate appropriate portions of his responsibilities to members of his organization, together with proportionate authority for their fulfillment, but he may not delegate or relinquish his overall responsibility for results or any portion of his accountability.

A. *Activities*
  1. Management Responsibilities
      a. Direct the activities of the Division to insure the security and optimum yield on invested capital, as well as optimum profits from operations and sales.
      b. Administer Company policy within the Division, consistent with the policies established by the President and the Board of Directors.
      c. Establish for each department, plant and region within the Division, and for the Division as such, operating and/ or profit objectives consistent with those set by the President.
      d. Establish and maintain friendly contacts and good public relations with leaders in local businesses, as well as in civic and governmental affairs.
  2. Control, Financial and Legal Responsibilities
      a. Implement all accounting policies and procedures established by the Vice President–Secretary-Treasurer, including the preparation of the financial and operating reports

as required by the Vice President–Secretary-Treasurer.
- *b.* Maintain effective systems of control over such activities as capital expenditures, operating expenses, disbursements, purchases, manpower utilization, wages, salaries and Company property.
- *c.* Review and approve all departmental, plant, region and Division operating budgets; advertising budgets; capital budgets; and charitable donations prior to submitting a consolidated budget(s) for the Division to the President for approval. Assume responsibility for the operation of the Division within the budget approved by the President.
- *d.* Maintain necessary personnel and facilities to properly safeguard Company property.
- *e.* Submit recommendations for insurance coverage to the Vice President–Secretary-Treasurer.
- *f.* Control level and content of the field warehouses and assembly plant inventories, taking into consideration optimum turnover, consistent with material availability, competitive conditions and marketing requirements.
- *g.* Submit to the Vice President–Secretary-Treasurer for approval all leases and legal contracts, other than contracts involving the normal course of day-to-day business and labor agreements.
- *h.* Submit requests for the employment or services of outside
  - (1) legal counsel,
  - (2) financial and/or other consultants, and
  - (3) professional or specialized services
    - (a) through the Vice President–Engineering to the President for approval on all engineering and patent matters,
    - (b) through the Vice President–Personnel Relations to the President for approval on all personnel and labor relations matters,
    - (c) through the Vice President–Secretary-Treasurer to the President for approval on all matters not pertaining to engineering, patents, personnel or labor relations.

3. Companywide Marketing Responsibilities
   - *a.* Formulate and supervise overall Company sales policies and procedures necessary to obtain the optimum volume of profitable sales of Company products.
   - *b.* Establish standard terms of sale for Company products. Obtain concurrence from Vice President–Secretary-Treas-

urer where the terms of payment (including cash discount) are extended beyond the established standard.

c. Establish minimum price levels on Company products, receiving the Division Manager's approval of prices offered below these minimums.

d. Conduct market research to determine market potential, penetration and requirement for Company products.

e. Provide respective Division Managers with detailed forecasts of anticipated sales of the Division's products.

f. Initiate plans for modifications of existing products and for new products to be marketed, including the function and quality levels. Recommend priority schedules to the Division Manager.

g. Function as the Company's chief spokesman in NEMA.

h. Select and supervise industrial design consultants for the styling and packaging of Company's products.

4. Marketing Division Responsibilities

a. Establish sales quotas for the domestic market consistent with the Company's sales objective established by the President.

b. Approve the establishment of regional and district territories, location of sales offices and the addition of any marketing facility.

c. Establish procedures and policies for the headquarters sales departments associated with Manufacturing Divisions, which will

   (1) aggressively promote and obtain the optimum sales of the Division's products;

   (2) work closely with the Division's manufacturing personnel, contributing to the efficiency and profitability of the Division;

   (3) keep the Division Manager informed of sales and customer requirements to insure the most favorable market position; and

   (4) conform to the Manufacturing Division's policy with respect to office rules, salary levels, benefits, etc.

d. Operate field warehouses, select sites and facilities, allocate space for divisional products, establish necessary procedures, prepare and administer expenses and capital budgets, select and direct personnel.

e. Select qualified distributors and agents for the promotion and sale of the Company's products and approve associated agreements.

      f. Select advertising agencies to be retained by the Company and supervise their relationship with the Company.

      g. Operate those Assembly plants assigned to the Marketing Division and be responsible for the profitable operation of these plants.

5. Manufacturing and Engineering Responsibilities

      a. Assure the maintenance of efficient manufacturing staff, facilities and methods to produce quality products at the lowest possible cost.

      b. Assure the maintenance of an effective and efficient engineering staff and facilities for the design of products to insure satisfaction of market requirements.

      c. Assume responsibility for compliance with established engineering and quality standards.

6. Industrial Relations and Personnel Responsibilities

      a. Formulate and execute necessary policies to develop and maintain good employee relations.

      b. Assume responsibility for negotiations of union agreements within the Division. Review and approve any contemplated change in existing personnel policies or labor agreements

      c. Oversee the administration of the pension, retirement and. group insurance programs in accordance with established policies.

      d. Submit to the President for approval recommendations for salary adjustments or assignments of management personnel who are on the first echelon below the Division Manager as well as the Regional Managers.

      e. Conduct periodic appraisals which shall judge the performance and potential ability of those reporting directly to him. Assume responsibility for similar appraisals being made of other supervisory personnel.

      f. Assume responsibility for the selection, training, upgrading and development of Division personnel. This will include the training of replacements qualified to fill vacancies when they occur in key management positions throughout the Division.

      g. Encourage and assist in the best possible communications with all employees to secure an informed, cooperative and efficient organization.

III. RELATIONSHIP TO OTHERS

    A. *President*

    He is accountable to the President for fulfillment of his functions and responsibilities. He will assist the President on any matter to which he is assigned.

B. *Division Managers*

He will maintain close liaison with other Division Managers to insure obtaining optimum sales of the Company's product.

C. *Division Personnel*

He is responsible for the supervision of those reporting directly to him; and they, in turn, will be responsible for the supervision of their subordinates within established policies.

D. *Vice President–Personnel Relations*

He will maintain close liaison with the Vice President–Personnel Relations, keeping him informed of the Division's plans and activities in this area of operation. He will consult with him and use his counsel and advice on plans, programs and procedures pertaining to personnel, labor and public relations.

E. *Vice President–Secretary-Treasurer*

He will maintain close liaison with the Vice President–Secretary-Treasurer, keeping him informed of the Division's plans and activities in this area of operation. He will consult with him and use his counsel and advice on plans involving financial and accounting matters.

F. *Vice President–Subsidiaries*

He will collaborate with the Vice President–Subsidiaries on marketing plans, activities, advertising and sales publication programs that could affect the export and subsidiary marketing effort and/or profitability of the Company.

G. *Division Manager–Regional Division*

He will maintain close liaison with the Division Manager–Regional Division, encouraging coordination of sales activities with other divisions to insure optimum sales performance throughout the Company.

MANAGER–MARKETING RESEARCH

I. FUNCTIONS

The Manager of Marketing Research is responsible for developing and supervising the Company's Marketing Research programs to help achieve the maximum volume of profitable sales.

He is responsible for carrying out all policies, procedures and programs indicated by the Vice President–Marketing, while insuring efficient operation of the Marketing Research Department.

II. RESPONSIBILITIES AND AUTHORITY

Within the limits of his approved program, Company policies and control procedures, the Marketing Research Manager is responsible for, and has commensurate authority to fulfill, the duties set forth herein. He may not delegate or relinquish his overall responsibility or any portion of his accountability.

A. *Activities*
  1. Staff Responsibilities to Vice President–Marketing
     a. Conduct studies to help formulate both short- and long-term plans and objectives for the growth and expansion of the Company's sales.
     b. Coordinate with appropriate members of Marketing Management on any studies of policies, methods or procedures to which assigned.
     c. Coordinate, initiate, review and recommend changes in the reports used to measure performance against the Company's marketing objectives.
     d. Conduct special studies to determine the effectiveness of individual marketing programs, as requested.
     e. Make periodic surveys of competitors' sales manpower and maintain a reference file of noncatalog information pertaining to principal competitors.
     f. Conduct necessary market analysis to provide an accurate measure of market potential and Company's position in the market.
     g. Administer, review and recommend changes to the Field Sales Bonus Plan and coordinate with the Controller–Marketing Division on any changes affecting the Field Sales Bonus Plan.
     h. Provide forecasts of anticipated business conditions in sufficient detail to reflect the outlook for each of the Company's significant product markets.
     i. Coordinate the Company's participation in NEMA statistical programs, maintain records pertaining thereto, report Company's market position to interested management members and participate in appropriate NEMA statistical committees.
     j. Coordinate the use of any external marketing research

or economic consulting services, as well as the collection of information from the field sales organization.

k. Coordinate the preparation and use of budgets within the Marketing Division and conduct special expense studies.

l. Maintain complete statistical records of orders and shipments, as well as a research library of government and other publications pertaining to markets and general business conditions.

m. Coordinate and administer the purchasing of Marketing Division forms and office equipment to insure obtaining the maximum quality and quantity for the minimum price.

n. Coordinate the preparation, publication and administration of Marketing Division policies, especially those affecting the field sales organization.

o. Maintain priority list of current assignments and periodically send it to the Vice President–Marketing for review and determination of any new priorities.

2. Marketing Responsibilities

a. Coordinate the preparation of sales quotas and, after approval of the Marketing Division Managers, supervise periodic reports of performance with respect to objectives.

b. Supply the Marketing Division Managers with information showing the natural boundaries of specific markets, their potential and Company's penetration, as required for decision on territory boundaries, location of sales offices and assignment of manpower.

c. Make periodic studies to determine the share of field selling effort directed to different types of customers and to ascertain the relative potential of different classes of trade.

d. Assist the Marketing Division Managers in the administration of Marketing policies directly affecting the field sales organization, such as automobile reimbursement and insurance and personnel transfers.

e. Conduct product studies as requested by the Product Manager to determine
(1) Customers' acceptance of existing products.
(2) Market requirements for new products.

3. Management, Control and Organization Responsibilities

a. Formulate and administer Market Research policy consistent with overall policies established by the Vice President–Marketing.

b. Coordinate Marketing Research activities through personnel situated at the various operating units of the Company.

c. Determine that all periodic or special reports desired by the Vice President–Marketing, or other members of management, are prepared as requested and submitted on schedule.

d. Prepare an annual budget for the Marketing Research Department for the approval of the Vice President–Marketing and be responsible for the operation of the Marketing Research Department within the approved budget.

e. Approve all expenditures up to $200, or as prescribed by other established policy, not exceeding the limit imposed by the Vice President–Marketing.

f. Establish and maintain a sound organization in the Marketing Research Department, initiating or recommending changes in the organizational structure and assignment of personnel, as necessary.

g. Recruit new Marketing Research employees and co-ordinate their training.

h. Submit to the Vice President–Marketing, for approval, recommendations for salary adjustments for personnel in the Marketing Research Department.

i. Promote and encourage the best possible communication with all employees to secure an informed, cooperative and efficient organization.

j. Conduct periodic appraisals which will judge the performance and potential ability of all personnel reporting to him.

k. Insure that personnel policies of the Marketing Research Department conform to the established policies of Corporate Headquarters.

III. RELATIONSHIP TO OTHERS

A. *Vice President–Marketing*
He is accountable to the Vice President–Marketing for fulfillment of his functions and responsibilities. He will serve in any manner prescribed or perform any task to which he is assigned.

B. *Marketing Division Managers, Product Manager and Product Sales Managers*
He will maintain close liaison with the various Sales Managers to assure maximum use of Marketing Research facilities in the fulfillment of their missions, as well as to obtain background information necessary to provide effective Marketing Research.

C. *Division Managers*

He will provide staff assistance on Marketing Research and any associated problems which might be raised by Division Managers or members of top management.

MANAGER–DISTRIBUTOR RELATIONS

I. Functions

The Manager–Distributor Relations is responsible to the Vice President–Marketing for the operation of the Company's distributor program in the 37 Eastern states.

He is directly charged with developing and executing the distributor policy of the Company, while, at the same time, maintaining a relationship between the Company and its distributors that will insure a pleasant and profitable operation for all concerned. This also entails working with and advising the field sales organization on the proper handling of the Authorized Distributor organization.

II. Responsibilities and Authority

Within the limits of his approved program and Company policies and control procedures, the Manager–Distributor Relations is responsible for, and has commensurate authority to accomplish, the fulfillment of his assigned responsibilities. He may delegate to members of his organization appropriate portions of his responsibility, together with proportionate authority for their fulfillment, but he may not delegate or relinquish his overall responsibility for results or any portion of his accountability.

A. *Activities*

1. Management Responsibilities

   a. Develop and direct the Company's distributor program to achieve maximum results from this marketing channel, consistent with the policies established by the Vice President–Marketing.

   b. Formulate and administer the Company's distributor policy under the guidance of the Vice President–Marketing and in cooperation with the Distributor Policy Committee.

   c. Establish and maintain a continuing review of both short-

and long-term plans for expansion of Company sales through wholesale distribution organizations.

    d. Select and direct the Authorized Distributor organization, within the limits established by the Vice President–Marketing.

    e. Under the guidance of the Vice President–Marketing, coordinate Company advertising and sales promotion activities whenever they pertain to the distributor program.

    f. Collaborate with the Product Sales Managers in the establishment of sales quotas for the Authorized Distributor organization, consistent with Company objectives and the capabilities of the Distributor organization.

    g. Collaborate with the field sales organization, through the General Sales Manager, to insure the maximum results from the sale of Company products through authorized distributors.

    h. Determine that all periodic or special reports desired by the Vice President–Marketing or other members of management are presented as requested and submitted on schedule.

    i. Approve all expenditures and credits to the distributor organization, whether they be due to return of material for credit, promotion allowances, sales policy decisions or any other reason.

    j. Maintain effective systems of control over such activities as NAED meetings and conventions, distributor training programs, distributor promotion meeting allowances, etc.

2. Marketing Responsibility

    a. Establish distribution policies and channels of sale, including the selection and removal of authorized distributors in accordance with policies established by the Vice President–Marketing.

    b. Advise and assist the field sales organization in the proper execution of the Company's distributor policy.

    c. Supervise the execution of the distributor policy to guarantee the maximum benefits therefrom, while maintaining the proper respect and harmony between the Company and the Authorized Distributor organization.

    d. Assist the Headquarters Sales Advertising Sections in the editing and distributing of house organs for the Authorized Distributor organization.

    e. Write a Distributor Memo Ad monthly for insertion in the *Electrical Wholesaling* magazine.

      f. Establish and coordinate a distributor training program with the Student Training Coordinators.

3. Product Planning Responsibilities

    Obtain from the field sales offices continuing reports on competitors' products, promotion programs and merchandising programs to keep the Vice President–Marketing and the Product Sales Managers abreast of competitive situations involving the Company's products sold through distributors.

4. Miscellaneous Responsibilities

    a. Maintain close contact and supervision with all personnel under his jurisdiction, to insure proper understanding of their problems and to assist in their training.

    b. Submit to the Vice President–Marketing, for approval. recommendations for salary adjustments in accordance with established procedures.

    c. Handle special assignments as directed by the Vice President–Marketing, including service on NAED committees and projects with other organizations outside the normal scope of activity.

III.   RELATIONSHIP TO OTHERS

    A. *Vice President–Marketing*

He is accountable to the Vice President–Marketing for the fulfillment of his functions and responsibilities. He will serve in an advisory capacity to the Vice President–Marketing on any matter to which he is assigned.

    B. *General Sales Manager*

He will maintain close liaison with the General Sales Manager so as to know the objectives and work with the field Marketing organization toward meeting these objectives.

    C. *Product Manager*

He will maintain close liaison with the Product Manager to insure maximum cooperation between the distributor organization and the Product Sales Managers.

    D. *Market Research Manager*

He will collaborate in the Market Research projects involving information concerning the Authorized Distributor organization or merchandise sales through this media.

    E. *Advertising Manager*

He will collaborate with the Advertising Manager on all advertising and sales projects promotion pertaining to the distributor organization.

DIVISION CONTROLLER

I. FUNCTIONS

The Division Controller is responsible for establishing sound accounting methods and procedures for use in the Marketing Division and Assembly Plants, consistent with the policies established by the Vice President–Secretary-Treasurer of the Company.

He will assist the Region Managers and such other accounting personnel as designated by the Region Managers to efficiently perform the accounting functions at each of the Region Assembly Plants.

He has direct supervision over, and is responsible for the efficient operation of, the following activities of the Marketing Division: General Accounting, salary and hourly payrolls, internal audits, systems and procedures, payroll tax functions, group insurance, automobile insurance, and lease administration.

II. RESPONSIBILITIES AND AUTHORITY

Within the limits of his approved program and Company policies and control procedures, the Division Controller is responsible for, and has commensurate authority to accomplish, the fulfillment of the duties set forth below. He may delegate to members of his organization appropriate portions of his responsibilities, together with proportionate authority for their fulfillment, but he may not delegate or relinquish his overall responsibility for results or any portion of his accountability.

A. *Activities*
   1. Management Responsibilities
      a. Supervise and assist various personnel reporting directly to the Division Controller in the fulfillment of their assigned duties.
      b. Assist Region Managers and other accounting personnel in the Region Assembly Plants to efficiently perform their accounting functions.
      c. Inspect periodically the accounting activities and procedures being followed at each Assembly Plant, ascertaining that these activities are being carried on in accordance with established policy, making recommendations for improvements to the Region Managers.
      d. Establish and effectuate the necessary measurement fac-

tors to control performance against approved plans and standards.

e. Issue and maintain adequate Standard Practice Bulletins necessary for proper correlation of the activities of the various units in the Division.

f. Supervise and direct all accounting systems and procedures work in the Division. This function will include preparation of or supervision of written accounting procedures to insure adherence to most efficient methods and for proper training and instruction of new employees.

g. Develop for approval by the Vice President–Division Manager-Marketing and advise the Vice President–Secretary-Treasurer of necessary burden rates to permit computation of proper costing of products.

2. Budget and Control Responsibilities

a. Maintain adequate records of authorized appropriations and determine that all sums expended pursuant thereto are properly accounted for.

b. Maintain an adequate system of internal control over cash receipts and disbursements and preparation and disbursement of payrolls.

c. Assist in preparing Assembly Plant operating budgets and capital expenditure budgets in cooperation with the Region Managers.

d. Determine that Divisional records are adequate to insure proper control over Company assets assigned to the Division.

e. Maintain appropriate records of inventory values and the supervision of physical inventories and their valuations.

f. Assure that all reports, within the jurisdiction of the Controller, are prepared in the prescribed manner and are submitted on schedule.

g. Prepare the annual budget for the department and be responsible to the Vice President–Division Manager-Marketing for the operation of the department within the approved budget.

h. Consolidate the entire Capital Expenditure Budget for the Division prior to forwarding the consolidated budget to the Vice President–Division Manager-Marketing for approval.

3. Forecast and Interpretation of Control Data

a. Interpret and administer Company financial and accounting policies.

   b. Prepare forecasts of cash requirements, financial condition and results of operation.

   c. Report and interpret results of operations of the Division to all levels of management.

  4. Insurance

   a. Recommend to the Vice President–Secretary-Treasurer any changes necessary to maintain proper insurance coverage of the properties and activities of the Division.

   b. Maintain appropriate records and administer the group insurance program.

   c. Maintain appropriate records and administer the automobile insurance program for the Division.

   d. Coordinate the preparation and filing of insurance claims for the recovery of damages, except claims under liability policies and under Workmen's Compensation insurance policies.

  5. Miscellaneous Responsibilities

   a. Submit statistical reports required by governmental agencies to the Vice President–Secretary-Treasurer for review and transmission to the agency involved.

   b. Maintain necessary records in connection with lease administration, reviewing leases for conformance with policy, advising management of renewals and terminations.

   c. Undertake such other related duties or specific assignments as may be directed by management.

   d. Conduct periodic appraisals of those employees reporting to him. The appraisal will judge in detail the individual results and methods. It will also include recommendations for further development of the individual.

   e. Encourage and assist in the best possible communication with all employees to secure an informed, cooperative and efficient organization.

III.   RELATIONSHIP TO OTHERS

  A.   *Vice President–Division Manager-Marketing*
  He is accountable to the Vice President–Division Manager-Marketing for the fulfillment of his functions and responsibilities. He will serve in an advisory capacity as required.

  B.   *Manager _____ Division and _____*
  He will work closely with the Managers to insure the maximum efficiency of the units of the Marketing and Assembly Divisions.

  C.   *Vice President–Secretary-Treasurer*
  He is accountable to the Vice President–Secretary-Treasurer for

adherence to accounting and financial policies, methods and procedures that may be established or approved by the Vice President–Secretary-Treasurer.

D. *Region Managers*

He will maintain close liaison with the Region Managers, providing assistance and counsel in those areas coming within the scope of the Division Controller.

E. *Assembly Plant Accountants and Office Managers of Assembly Plants*

He will, through the Region Manager, oversee the activities of the Plant Accountants and Office Managers to ascertain that the accounting and financial policies, methods and procedures, as established by the Controller, are being followed.

GENERAL SALES MANAGER

I. FUNCTIONS

The General Sales Manager is responsible to the Vice President–Marketing for field marketing operations in 37 states.

He is charged directly with executing such policies, procedures and programs as may be indicated by the Vice President–Marketing, while insuring efficient operation of the _____ Field Marketing Organization and assisting toward the objective of maximum volume of profitable sales.

II. RESPONSIBILITIES AND AUTHORITY

Within the limits of his approved program and Company policies and control procedures, the General Sales Manager is responsible for, and has commensurate authority to accomplish, the fulfillment of his assigned responsibilities. He may delegate to members of his own staff appropriate portions of his responsibilities, together with proportionate authority for their fulfillment, but he may not delegate or relinquish his overall responsibility for results or any portion of his accountability.

Activities

1. Management Responsibilities

   a. Through Region Managers operate the _____ Field Marketing Organization efficiently and within limits established by the Vice President–Marketing to obtain maximum volume of profitable sales for all Divisions of the Company.

    b. Formulate and administer sales policy as it pertains to field office operations and Assembly Plants, consistent with the policies established by the Vice President–Marketing.

    c. Collaborate with other marketing personnel in the establishment of sales quotas consistent with Company objectives and sales office capabilities.

    d. Establish for each Region sales expense and Assembly Plant budgets consistent with the objectives set by the Vice President–Marketing.

    e. Establish and maintain a continuing review of both short- and long-term plans for expansion of Company sales and develop the field sales and Assembly Plant capability to proportionate strength.

    f. Supervise and assist individuals reporting directly to him, delegating proportionate authority to carry out these assigned responsibilities.

2. Control and Financial Responsibilities

    a. Determine that all periodic or special reports desired by the Vice President–Marketing or other members of management are prepared as requested and submitted on schedule.

    b. Maintain effective systems of control over such general activities as capital expenditures, operating expenditures and results, manpower utilization, salaries and Company property within the jurisdiction of the _____ Field Marketing Organization.

    c. Approve all expenditures as prescribed by established policy without exceeding the limit imposed by the Vice President–Marketing.

    d. Provide for the necessary protection of Company property within his control, including responsibility for notifying the appropriate Division Controller or the Vice President–Secretary-Treasurer of risks to be covered by insurance.

    e. Prepare and submit to the Vice President–Marketing for approval all annual operating budgets and requests for capital expenditures within the jurisdiction of the _____ Field Marketing Organization.

    f. Collaborate with other Marketing personnel in the development of coming year's advertising budget for the parent Company, subject to review and approval of the Vice President–Marketing.

3. Organization Responsibilities

    Establish and maintain a sound organizational structure in the _____ Field Marketing Organization, including changes in organizational structure and assignment of personnel.

    4. Marketing Responsibilities

       a. Supervise the operation of the _____ Field Sales Offices and Assembly Plants, including selection and administration of personnel involved.

       b. Assist in establishing distribution policies and channels of sale, including the selection and approval of distributors. Serve as Chairman of the Distributor Policy Committee.

PRODUCT MANAGER

I. FUNCTIONS

The Product Manager is responsible to the Vice President–Marketing for the overall supervision and efficient operation of the Marketing Division Product Sales Departments in a manner which is compatible with obtaining the maximum volume of profitable sales.

He is charged with executing policies, procedures, and programs, as established by the Vice President–Marketing.

II. RESPONSIBILITIES AND AUTHORITY

Within the limits of his approved program and the Company policies and control procedures, the Product Manager is responsible for, and has commensurate authority to accomplish, the fulfillment of his assigned responsibilities. He may delegate to members of his organization appropriate portions of his responsibilities, together with proportionate authority for their fulfillment, but he may not delegate or relinquish his overall responsibility for results or any portion of his accountability.

    A. Activities

      1. Management Responsibilities

        a. Establish, consistent with the policies established by the Vice President–Marketing, those programs and procedures for each Product Sales Department which will assist the field organization in obtaining the optimum volume of profitable sales of each division's products.

        b. Review and approve sales quotas recommended by the respective Product Sales Managers before submitting these recommendations to the Vice President–Marketing for approval.

        c. Continually evaluate competitive conditions, technical

advances, and market potentials, recommending extent of participation, design changes, and both short- and long-range product development.

    d. Supervise and assist individuals reporting directly to him, delegating proportionate authority to carry out their assigned responsibilities.

    e. Assist in the formulation and establishment of advertising, marketing, and sales promotion programs for the Company's products.

    f. Coordinate large job and/or systems activity and negotiation.

    g. Exercise general supervision through the respective Product Sales Managers over the operation of the Product Sales Department, including selection and administration of personnel involved.

    h. Establish and maintain a uniform product service procedure which will provide product service by the Divisions or manufacturing plants consistent with the best interest of the Company and its customers.

2. Control and Financial Responsibilities

    a. Review and approve expense and capital equipment budgets, as prepared by the Product Sales Managers, before submitting these budgets to the Vice President–Marketing for approval. He is responsible for operating within approved budgets.

    b. Approve all expenditures, as prescribed by other established policy, not exceeding limits imposed by the Vice President–Marketing.

    c. Provide for necessary protection of Company property within his control.

3. Marketing Responsibilities

    a. Establish, consistent with the price policies set by the Vice President–Marketing, the criteria by which the Product Sales Managers establish the price levels for their respective divisions' or manufacturing plants' products. Obtain Manufacturing Division or Manufacturing Plant Manager's approval of prices offered below the established minimum price level.

    b. Assist, through membership on the Distributor Policy Committee, in the establishment of distributor policies and channels of sales, including selection and approval of distributors.

      c. Coordinate Product Sales Departments' activities with the Marketing Division Managers to obtain the maximum effectiveness of the overall marketing effort.

4. Product Planning and Engineering Responsibilities
   a. Review and approve each Product Sales Manager's program on new products to be marketed and desired modifications to existing products.
   b. Keep abreast of developments and manufacturing programs directly related to product planning, advising the Product Sales Manager when alternative action should be taken.
   c. Collaborate with Marketing Division Managers to obtain maximum effectiveness of promotional plans involving products.
   d. Assure the maintenance of an effective and efficient application engineering staff, within each Product Sales Department, capable of meeting the marketing requirements.
   e. Determine, in conjunction with the Product Sales Manager, what action is required to correct field problems arising out of product failure, quality, or customer service, working out corrective measures with the appropriate members of the Manufacturing Division or Manufacturing Plant.
   f. Establish training program at Headquarters Sales Department for sales personnel, as well as for distributors and customers.

5. Personnel Responsibilities
   a. Develop and maintain a sound organization in each of the Product Sales Departments.
   b. Submit recommendations for personnel changes and salary adjustments to the Vice President–Marketing for approval, in accordance with established procedures.
   c. Conduct periodic appraisals which will judge the performance and potential ability of those employees reporting directly to him. Assume responsibility through delegated channels for similar appraisals' being made of other supervisory personnel.
   d. Encourage and assist in the best possible communication with all employees to secure an informed, cooperative, and efficient organization.

III. RELATIONSHIP TO OTHERS

    A. *Vice President–Marketing*
        He is accountable to the Vice President–Marketing for fulfillment of his functions, responsibilities, and assigned duties.

    B. *Managers–Marketing Division*
        He will maintain close liaison with the Marketing Division Managers to insure the optimum coordination between headquarters and the field marketing organization.

    C. *Marketing Division Staff*
        He will collaborate with other members of the Vice President–Marketing's staff to insure that the Division is meeting the commercial requirements consistent with profitable operations.

    D. *Division and Manufacturing Plant Managers*
        He will work closely with the Managers of the Manufacturing Division and Plants to insure compatibility of the Marketing Headquarters Departments with their operations, objectives, and Company goals.

    E. *Vice President–Manufacturing*
        He will coordinate with the Vice President–Manufacturing with respect to Product Planning and Product Development activity commercially desirable to meet Company objectives.

DIVISION CONTROL SALES MANAGER *

I. FUNCTIONS

The _____ Control Sales Manager is responsible to the Product Manager–Marketing Division for _____ Headquarters Sales Department operations and associated activity, both at headquarters and in the field, with the objective of obtaining maximum volume of profitable sales.

He is charged directly with executing such policies, procedures and programs as may be indicated by the Product Manager–Marketing Division, while insuring efficient operation of the _____ Headquarters Sales Department compatible with the best interests of the stockholders, the employees and customer service.

---

*At the request of this company, the division is not identified here.

II. Responsibilities and Authority

Within the limits of his approved program and the Company policies and control procedures, the _____ Control Sales Manager is responsible for, and has commensurate authority to accomplish, the fulfillment of his assigned responsibilities. He may delegate, to members of his own organization, appropriate portions of his responsibilities, together with proportionate authority for their fulfillment, but he may not delegate or relinquish his overall responsibility for results or any portion of his accountability.

A. *Activities*

1. Management Responsibilities
   a. Operate the _____ Headquarters Sales Department efficiently and within limits established by the Product Manager–Marketing Division.
   b. Establish and maintain a continuing review of both short- and long-term plans for the expansion of Company sales of _____ control.
   c. Submit to the Vice President–Marketing through the Product Manager–Marketing forecasts of future business which will assist in the formulation of recommendations to the _____ Division Manager in planning and establishing his future operational programs.
   d. Submit to the _____ Division Manager and/or his delegates operational requirements which should be met to insure the most favorable market position for the Company.

2. Control and Financial Responsibilities
   a. Determine that all periodic or special reports desired by the Product Manager–Marketing Division are prepared as requested and submitted on schedule.
   b. Maintain effective systems of control over such general activities as capital expenditures, operating expenditures and results, manpower utilization, salaries and Company property within the jurisdiction of the _____ Headquarters Sales Department.
   c. Prepare and submit to the Product Manager–Marketing Division for approval expense budgets and capital requirements for all operations within the scope of his responsibility. Be responsible for operating within approved budget.
   d. Approve all expenditures as prescribed by other established policy—not exceeding limits imposed by the Product Manager–Marketing Division.

   e. Provide for the necessary protection of Company property within his control, including the responsibility for notifying the _____ Division Controller of risks to be covered by insurance.

   f. Administer the Terms of Sale established for _____ control.

3. Marketing Responsibilities

   a. Establish and maintain a sound organizational structure in the _____ Headquarters Sales Department, including changes in organizational structure and assignment of personnel so that all customer orders can be processed in a minimum amount of time and that Application Engineering can be scheduled for completion to meet customer delivery requirements.

   b. Supervise the operation of the _____ Headquarters Sales Department, including selection and administration of personnel involved.

   c. Assist in the establishment of distribution policies and channels of sale, including selection and approval of distributors through membership on the Distributor Policy Committee.

   d. Establish minimum prices, as approved by the Vice President–Marketing, for the Division's products. Approval by the Division Manager is necessary for prices below these levels.

   e. Work with Corporate Advertising in the preparation of rough copy, cataloging, sales promotion publications, product stories, application pictures and ad layouts of the _____ Division products.

   f. Maintain necessary mailing lists and make distribution of catalogs and sales promotion publications.

   g. Assist in the development of attractive and functional product exhibits for use at trade shows and handle headquarters arrangements for shows as assigned.

   h. Cooperate with Regional Managers and Marketing Research in establishing sales territory quotas.

   i. Prepare for release, through Corporate Advertising, all product publicity to trade papers.

   j. Survey and study competitors' products, advertising and promotion programs, and price policy to keep abreast of competitive trends involving _____ control (keeping the Product Manager–Marketing Division and the _____ Division Manager informed).

    k. Develop merchandising programs to stimulate the Company's sales of _____ control.

    l. Collaborate with the Marketing Research Manager in studies necessary to provide accurate measurement of market potential and the _____ Division's position in the market.

    m. Establish training programs on _____ control equipment for Company sales personnel, as well as for distributors and customers.

    n. Be responsible for competitive relationship pertinent to _____ control.

    o. Process all requests for field service and cooperate with the Chief Engineer to insure that the scheduling of customer service for start-up or breakdown is arranged to provide maximum overall customer satisfaction and minimum disruption of other activities of the _____ Division.

4. Product Planning Responsibilities

    a. Determine new _____ control products to be marketed and recommend desirable modifications to existing products, including functions and quality levels. Submit to _____ Division approved Marketing Division priority schedules.

    b. Through the _____ Division Manager and/or his delegates, keep abreast of all development and manufacturing programs directly related to product planning, advising the _____ Division Manager when timing is detrimental to commercial interest.

5. Personnel Responsibilities

    a. Insure that personnel policies of the _____ Headquarters Sales Department conform, where necessary, to the policies established by the _____ Division with respect to housekeeping, salary schedules, rates, etc.

    b. Submit to the Product Manager–Marketing Division for approval recommendations for salary adjustments, in accordance with established procedures.

    c. Maintain close contact with all personnel under his jurisdiction to insure proper understanding of their problems and to assist in their training.

    d. Conduct periodic appraisals of the personnel reporting to him. These appraisals shall judge in detail the individual's results and methods; will also include recommendations for further development of the individual. He will, in turn, be responsible for seeing that similar appraisals are maintained for all personnel under his jurisdiction.

III. RELATIONSHIP TO OTHERS

A. *Product Manager–Marketing Division*

He is accountable to the Product Manager–Marketing Division for fulfillment of his functions and responsibilities. He will serve as staff to the Product Manager–Marketing Division on _____ control marketing matters or any others to which he is assigned from time to time.

B. *Department Heads*

He will maintain close liaison with other _____ Division Department Heads to insure maximum cooperation in product planning, establishment of finished-goods inventory, scheduling to meet customer delivery requirements, and any other matters that will contribute to the success of the _____ Division.

C. *Managers–Marketing Division (Regional)*

He will collaborate with the Marketing Division Managers to insure short lines of communication and the best possible coordination between the headquarters and field sales organization, as well as maximum effectiveness from the Company's advertising and sales promotion involving _____ control.

D. *Marketing Research Manager*

He will collaborate in marketing research involving _____ control.

DIVISION MARKETING MANAGER*

I. FUNCTIONS

The _____ Industry Marketing Manager has as his responsibility the sales coordination and promotion of all Company products to _____ Industry to attain the maximum volume of profitable sales. Reporting

---

*At the request of this company, the division is not identified here.

directly to the Product Manager, he is responsible for carrying out all policies, procedures and programs to which he is assigned.

II. Responsibilities and Authority

Within the limits of his approved program and Company policies and control procedures, the _____ Industry Marketing Manager is responsible for, and has commensurate authority to accomplish, the fulfillment of his assigned responsibilities.

A. *Activities*
1. Coordinate large job and system activity specifically involving _____ industry. Assist on individual job transactions.
2. Establish and maintain a continuing review of both short- and long-term plans for new products and systems utilized in _____ industry.
3. Assist _____ Industry Control Sales Manager in his product planning activity.
4. Establish and maintain a continuing review of _____ industry quotations and jobs, taking necessary action to insure an increasing amount of profitable business for the Company.
5. Coordinate with the Product Sales Managers in the development and execution of promotional and training programs directed toward _____ industry.
6. Working through the Regional Managers, coordinate Regional Engineer activity with _____ industry customers.
7. Prepare and submit to the Product Manager for approval an annual budget for his operations and be responsible for operation within the approved budget.

III. Relationship to Others

A. *Product Manager–Marketing Division*
He is accountable to the Product Manager–Marketing Division for fulfillment of his functions and responsibilities.
B. *Product Sales Managers*
He will collaborate and coordinate with the Product Sales Managers in his activities in their areas of responsibility.
C. *Managers–Marketing Division*
He will coordinate his field activities with the Marketing Division Managers to achieve maximum effectiveness.
D. *Regional Managers*
He will coordinate with the Regional Managers in his field activities coming within the scope of their operations.

MANAGER–REGIONAL DIVISION*

I. FUNCTIONS

The Manager of the _____ Division is responsible to the Vice President–Marketing for all field marketing operations within the authorized boundaries of the _____ Division.

He is charged directly with executing such policies, procedures, and programs as may be established by the Vice President–Marketing, while ensuring efficient operation of the _____ Division and assisting toward the objective of maximum volume of profitable sales.

II. RESPONSIBILITIES AND AUTHORITY

Within the limits of his approved program and Company policies and control procedures, the Manager of the _____ Division is responsible for, and has commensurate authority to accomplish, the fulfillment of his assigned responsibilities. He may delegate to members of his own staff appropriate portions of his responsibilities, together with proportionate authority for their fulfillment, but he may not delegate or relinquish his overall responsibility for results or any portion of his accountability.

A. *Activities*

1. Management Responsibilities
   a. Through Region Managers, operate the _____ Division efficiently and within the limits established by the Vice President–Marketing to obtain the maximum volume of profitable sales for all products of the Company.
   b. Formulate and administer sales policy as it pertains to field sales office, warehouse, and Assembly Plant operations, consistent with the policies established by the Vice President–Marketing.
   c. Coordinate with Marketing Research personnel in the establishment of sales quotas consistent with Company objectives as established by the Vice President–Marketing.
   d. Coordinate with Marketing Research and Marketing Accounting personnel in the establishment of expense budgets for all field sales offices, warehouses, and Assembly Plants within the _____ Division consistent with Marketing objectives as established by the Vice President–Marketing.

---

*At the request of this company, the division is not identified here.

e. Establish and maintain a continuing review of both short- and long-term plans for expansion of Company sales and develop the field sales, warehouse, and Assembly Plant capabilities to proportionate strength.

f. Supervise and assist individuals reporting directly to him, delegating proportionate authority to carry out these assigned responsibilities.

g. Collaborate with Manager of the _____ Division and Marketing Division staff to ensure attaining the maximum of profitable sales for entire Company.

2. Control and Financial Responsibilities

a. Determine that all periodic or special reports desired by the Vice President–Marketing or other members of management are prepared as requested and submitted on schedule.

b. Maintain effective systems of control over such general activities as capital expenditures, operating expenditures and results, manpower utilization, salaries, and Company property within the jurisdiction of the _____ Division.

c. Approve all expenditures as prescribed by established policy without exceeding the limit imposed by the Vice President–Marketing.

d. Provide for the necessary protection of Company property within his control, including responsibility for notifying the Division Controller or the Vice President–Secretary-Treasurer of risks to be covered by insurance.

e. Prepare, and submit to the Vice President–Marketing for approval, all annual operating budgets and requests for capital expenditures within the jurisdiction of the _____ Division.

3. Organizational Responsibilities

a. Maintain a sound organizational structure in the _____ Division and recommend any necessary changes in organizational structure, territorial boundaries, and assignment of personnel to the Vice President–Marketing for his approval.

4. Marketing Responsibilities

a. Supervise all operations of the _____ Division, including field sales office, warehouse, and Assembly Plant operations.

b. Assist in the selection and approval of distributors, as well as establishing distribution policies and channels of sale. Serve as Chairman of the Distributor Policy Committee for the _____ Division.

    c. Develop sales promotion programs to stimulate sales in various product lines and/or geographical areas and assist in the execution of such programs approved by the Product Manager and the Vice President–Marketing.

    d. Assist in obtaining from field offices and customers product stories and application pictures suitable for use in advertising, sales promotion bulletins, house organs, and publicity releases.

    e. Keep abreast of trends in advertising media and recommend to the Product Manager and Advertising Manager publications believed to be of interest.

    f. Coordinate with the Marketing Research Manager in the conduct of territorial and manpower analyses and in marketing research projects designed to provide accurate measurement of market potential, the Company's position in the market, customers' acceptance of products, and market requirements for new products.

    g. Coordinate with Product Manager on training programs for sales personnel and for distributors and customers.

    h. Obtain from the field sales offices continuing reports on competitors' products, promotion programs, and prices to keep the Vice President–Marketing and the Product Manager abreast of competitive situations involving the Company's products.

5. Personnel Responsibilities

    a. Insure that the personnel policies applied to personnel conform, insofar as practical, to policies established by the Plant in which they are located with respect to housekeeping, salary schedules, rates, etc.

    b. Submit to the Vice President–Marketing for approval recommendations for salary adjustments in accordance with established procedure.

    c. Maintain close contact with all personnel under his jurisdiction to insure proper understanding of their problems and to assist in their training.

    d. Conduct periodic appraisals of the personnel reporting to him. These appraisals will judge in detail the individual's results and methods and will also include recommendations for further development of the individual. He will, in turn, be responsible for seeing that similar appraisals are maintained for all supervisory personnel under his jurisdiction.

    e. Encourage and assist in the best possible communication with all employees to secure an informed, cooperative, and efficient organization.

III. Relationship to Others

  A. *Vice President–Marketing*
   He is accountable to the Vice President–Marketing for fulfillment of his functions and responsibilities. He will serve in an advisory capacity the Vice President–Marketing on any matter to which he is assigned.

  B. *Product Manager–Marketing Division*
   He will maintain close liaison with the Product Manager so as to know the Company's objectives and direct the field offices toward meeting them, while keeping the Product Manager informed of the field sales organization's product needs. He will assist in formulation and execution of sales promotion programs.

  C. *Marketing Division Staff*
   He will coordinate with other members of the Vice President–Marketing's staff to help insure the _____ Division is meeting sales needs consistent with profitable operations.

  D. *Vice President–Manufacturing*
   He will function as staff to the Vice President–Marketing on field sales questions and problems which might be raised by the Vice President–Manufacturing or other members of top management.

  E. *Vice President–Personnel Relations*
   He will maintain close liaison with the Vice President–Personnel Relations, keeping him informed on warehouse and Assembly Plant activities and plans. He will consult with him and use his counsel and advice on plans, programs and procedures pertaining to personnel and public relations.

  F. *Manager–_____ Division*
   He will coordinate with the Manager _____ Division on all field sales, warehouse and Assembly Plant operations which affect both the _____ Divisions.

REGION MANAGER

I. Functions

The Region Manager is the chief administrative and operating executive of the Region and, as such, has direct supervision over, and is responsible for the efficient management of, all departments within the Region, as well as all functions and facilities placed within the scope of the Region's operations.

He is directly charged with the responsibility of insuring the profitable operations of the Region compatible with the best interests of the stockholders, the employees and customer service.

He is responsible for the introduction and supply of products that will satisfy customer needs in the Region commensurate with established profit objectives.

II.   RESPONSIBILITIES AND AUTHORITY

Within the limits of his approved program and company policies and control procedures, the Region Manager is responsible for, and has commensurate authority to accomplish, the fulfillment of the duties set forth below. He may delegate to members of his organization appropriate responsibilities, together with proportionate authority for their fulfillment, but he may not delegate or relinquish his overall responsibility for results or any portion of his accountability.

A.   *Activities*

1.   Management Responsibilities

   a. Administer Company policy within the Region consistent with the policies established by the Vice President, Marketing and the Manager, _____ Division, as applicable.

   b. Establish and maintain a continuing review of both short- and long-term plans for market development, the growth of facilities and the introduction of new products within the Region, coordinated with other Regions through the Manager, _____ Division, as applicable.

   c. Supervise and assist employees reporting directly to him in the fulfillment of their assigned duties.

   d. Insure the achievement of operating and profit objectives established by the Vice President, Marketing.

   e. Establish and maintain friendly contacts and good public relations with leaders in the electrical industry and other industries and businesses, as well as in civic and governmental affairs.

2.   Control and Financial Responsibilities

   a. Insure that all periodic or special reports desired by the Management are prepared in suitable form and submitted on schedule.

   b. Maintain an effective accounting system, following the procedures established by the Controller–Marketing Division, which will truly reflect the financial condition of the operation.

   c. Maintain effective systems of control over such general activities as capital expenditures, operating expenses, sales expenses, sales engineering, purchases, production, personnel, wages and salaries.

   d. Recommend for Management approval all operating budgets, tooling budgets, requests for capital expenditures and charitable donations for each activity in the Region. Assume responsibility for the operation of the Region within the budget approved by the Vice President.

   e. Maintain effective control over purchase commitments, as well as the level and content of all inventories within the "A" plants, taking into consideration optimum turnover consistent with material availability and competitive conditions.

   f. Establish the level and content of stock to be maintained in field warehouses under his jurisdiction, subject to the approval of the Vice President, Marketing, and the Manager, _____ Division, as applicable.

   g. Maintain necessary personnel and facilities to safeguard all Company property.

   h. Recommend insurance coverage, if needed, to Marketing Division Controller.

   i. Be familiar with tax structure affecting Region and recommend to the Manager, _____ Division, as applicable, any action to be taken in regard thereto. Investigate tax liabilities incurred when opening a new sales office or facility.

   j. Approve all expenditures as prescribed by established policy without exceeding the limit imposed by the Vice President, Marketing.

3. Organizational Responsibilities

   a. Establish and maintain a sound organizational structure in the Region and recommend any necessary changes in organizational structure, territorial boundaries and assignment of personnel.

   b. Recommend the introduction and installation of new techniques and methods of management within the Region.

4. Marketing Responsibilities

   a. Exercise, through Area Sales Managers (where applicable), overall supervision pertaining to the entire marketing effort within the Region.

   b. Review established price levels on new and existing standard products. Where profit level is adversely affected to a significant degree, submit recommendations to the Vice President, Marketing, and the Manager, _____ Division, as applicable.

   c. Collaborate with the Product Manager–Marketing Division on establishment of minimum price levels for special products offered for sale in the Region. Approve prices offered for such products.

   d. Coordinate with the Product Manager–Marketing Division on modifications, changes or additions to existing product lines, considering market requirements and recommendations made by Engineering Departments.

   e. Maintain a sound Redistribution Warehouse organization in the Region.

   f. Coordinate with Product Manager and Manager, _____ Division, as applicable, on training programs for sales personnel, distributors and customers.

   g. Assist in establishing distribution policies and channels of sale, including the selection of distributors.

 5. Manufacturing and Engineering Responsibilities

   a. Maintain a manufacturing staff, facilities and methods to produce quality products at the lowest overall cost.

   b. Maintain an adequate engineering staff and facilities to design special products to satisfy the best possible market acceptance consistent with low cost.

   c. Assume responsibility for compliance of manufactured products with appropriate codes and ordinances, as well as recognized engineering standards and quality control.

 6. Industrial Relations and Personnel Responsibilities

   a. Formulate and administer necessary policies to develop and maintain good employee relations consistent with policies established by the Manager, _____ Division, as applicable.

   b. Assume responsibility for the hiring, firing, training, upgrading and development of personnel, consistent with policies and procedures established by the Vice President, Marketing.

   Where field sales personnel are involved, the hiring, firing and assignment of such personnel will be made by the Vice President, Marketing.

   c. Assume responsibility for administration of union labor contracts in the Assembly Plant or warehouses. Coordinate all matters prior to taking action with the Vice President, Personnel Relations.

    d. Review, and submit for approval, any contemplated change in existing personnel policies or labor contracts.

    e. Oversee the administration of the pension, retirement and insurance programs in conjunction with the Manager, _____ Division, as applicable.

    f. Review and recommend for approval all changes in wages and salaries.

    g. Conduct periodic appraisals which will judge the performance and potential ability of all supervisory personnel in the Region.

    h. Encourage and assist in the best possible communications with all employees to secure an informed, cooperative and efficient organization.

  7. Miscellaneous Responsibilities

    a. Recommend to the Manager, _____ Division, as applicable, possible channels which might profitably expand the market for the Company's growth and fully investigate such recommendations when requested to do so.

III.   Relationship to Others

***   *A.*   *Manager, _____ Division*
Is directly accountable to the Manager, _____ Division, as applicable, for the satisfactory fulfillment of all functions and responsibilities, as well as for the performance of any special duties he may assign.

  B.   *Product Manager–Marketing Division*
Collaborate with the Product Manager–Marketing Division in the development of promotional and merchandising programs to stimulate the sales of products and other allied equipment. Insure that price policies and terms of sale policies of the various product Divisions are properly administered. Assume responsibility for the quality level of special products manufactured by the Assembly Plant which incorporate products of the other Divisions. Administer engineering and construction standards of special products as formulated by the Divisions.

  C.   *Marketing Research Manager*
Collaborate with the Marketing Research Manager in conducting

---

*** indicates addition or revision

field surveys. Recommend changes for establishing proper coverage of local marketing areas. Assist in the preparation of Region and District Sales objectives to accomplish the Company's overall objectives.

D. *Controller–Marketing Division*

Coordinate with the Controller–Marketing Division on matters pertaining to the Region to insure satisfactory overall results, as well as economic accounting and control of operations.

E. *Region Managers*

Cooperate with other Region Managers to attain maximum sales and maximum and efficient use of all Assembly Plant facilities.

F. *Vice President–Personnel Relations*

Coordinate with the Vice President–Personnel Relations, keeping him informed on Assembly Plant and warehouse labor relations. Use his counsel and advice in all negotiations of union contracts.

G. *Distributor Relations Manager*

Coordinate with the Distributor Relations Manager on all matters pertaining to Distributors and Distribution within the Region, keeping him fully informed on Distributor Relations.

H. *Corporate Advertising Manager*

Collaborate with Corporate Advertising Manager on matters pertaining to advertising, sales promotions, shows, exhibits, local promotion, Company publications and related advertising activities.

*** I. *Other Members of Marketing Division Management*

Coordinate with other members of Marketing Division Management to insure that the Region is meeting sales needs consistent with profitable operations.

AREA SALES MANAGER

I. FUNCTIONS

The Area Sales Manager assumes overall responsibility for the performance of the several territories making up a Sales Area. Reporting directly to the Region Manager, he is the link through which top management maintains close and frequent contact with members of the field organization and their customers.

*** indicates addition or revision

II. Responsibilities and Authority

Within the limits of his approved program and Company policies and control procedures, the Area Sales Manager is responsible for, and has commensurate authority to accomplish, the fulfillment of the duties set forth below. He may delegate to members of his organization appropriate portions of his responsibility, together with proportionate authority for their fulfillment, but he may not delegate or relinquish his overall responsibilities for results or any portion of his accountability.

A. Activities

1. Management Responsibilities:
   a. Administer Company policy within the Sales Area consistent with the policies established by the Region Manager and the Marketing Division.
   b. Establish and maintain a continuing review of both short- and long-term plans for the growth of facilities and the introduction of new products within the Sales Area.
   c. Supervise and assist employees reporting directly to him in the fullfillment of their assigned duties.
   d. Assist the Region Manager in the achievement of operating and profit objectives of the Assembly Plant.
   e. Assist the Region Manager in the operation of warehouses not located at the Region Headquarters.

2. Control and Financial Responsibilities
   a. Insure that all periodic or special reports desired by the Region Manager are prepared in suitable form and submitted on schedule.
   b. Submit to the Region Manager recommended budgets for the territories under Area jurisdiction. Assume responsibility for operations, within the limits established by the Marketing Division.
   c. Analyze and approve Office and Travel Expense Statements submitted by personnel under his jurisdiction. This responsibility should not be delegated except when absolutely necessary. Persons authorized to act on such matters in the Area Sales Manager's absence must be approved by the Region Manager.

      Expense Statements executed by the Area Sales Manager must be approved by the Region Manager or General Sales Manager in the Region Manager's absence.
   d. Analyze all proposals involving changes in size and loca-

tion of field offices, making appropriate recommendations through the Region Manager to the office of the General Sales Manager.

- *e.* Conduct a continuing review of field office operations through inspection trips, reports and copies of correspondence—taking corrective action as required.

  Copies of inspection trip reports should be written to the Region Manager, with copies to the General Sales Manager. Distribution to the manager of the field office involved is optional.

- *f.* Assist on individual job transactions when they assume an unfavorable pattern. Otherwise, field offices may go direct to the Headquarters Sales Departments for decisions as to price level, delivery or other conditions of order acceptance.

- *g.* Cooperate with Division Headquarters Sales personnel, especially product specialists, in coordination of field trips and specific promotional activities to insure best results.

- *h.* Insure that all territories within the Sales Area promptly submit Expense Statements, Field Activity Summaries, Work Plans and other reports as required.

3. Organizational Responsibilities

- *a.* Establish and maintain a sound organizational structure in the Sales Area. Review and submit for approval all requests for changes in the organizational structure.

- *b.* Recommend the introduction and installation of new techniques and methods of management within the Sales Area.

4. Marketing Responsibilities

- *a.* Through the District Managers, exercise supervision and direction of Area Sales personnel. Recommend to the Region Manager any changes regarding personnel, including hiring, firing, job assignments, promotions and merit increases.

- *b.* Prepare sales quotas for the territories within the Sales Area, subject to review and approval of the Region Manager, using objectives established by the Marketing Division.

- *c.* Be responsible for execution of Headquarters-approved promotional plans, as well as an evaluation of their effectiveness. Also initiate local promotional programs.

- *d.* Make a continuing study of market potential and ways of getting increased business at reasonable expense.

- *e.* Report to the interested Marketing Headquarters all

significant trends in product acceptance, new markets and competitve activity.

   f. Work with field engineers (particularly the younger ones) under his jurisdiction and help with training in effective sales methods.

   g. Work with District Managers and help in their training as managers. Help in guiding them to get the management and sales job accomplished.

   h. Conduct sales meetings, as required, with field engineers and office personnel. Also conduct District or Sales Area meetings as soon as practical after Field Marketing Manager conferences.

   i. Through frequent contact, evaluate the effectiveness of authorized distributor organization, recommending desirable additions or deletions through the Distributor Relations Manager to the Distributor Policy Committee.

   j. Maintain occasional contact with all key accounts in the Sales Area.

5. Personnel Responsibilities

   a. Forward all matters pertaining to employee status, benefits, etc. to the Region Manager—making recommendations where appropriate.

   b. Conduct a continuing review of compensation levels and recommend to the Region Manager any desirable changes.

   c. Recommend to the Region Manager any necessary additions to the sales organization or office staff.

   d. Maintain close contact with all personnel under his jurisdiction to insure a proper understanding of their problems.

   e. Direct the Region Engineer's activities in his Sales Area (where applicable).

   f. Make sure the proper interpretations are put on the communications emanating from the various headquarters.

III. Relationships

   A. *Region Manager–Marketing Division*
Be directly accountable to the Region Manager–Marketing Division for the satisfactory fulfillment of all functions and responsibilities, as well as for the performance of any special duties he may assign.

   B. *Product Manager–Marketing Division*
Collaborate with the Product Manager–Marketing Division in the development of promotional and merchandising programs

to stimulate the sales of products and other allied equipment. Insure that the price policies and terms of sale policies of the various product Divisions are properly administered.

C. *Market Research Manager–Marketing Division*
Collaborate with the Market Research Manager–Marketing Division in conducting field surveys. Recommend through the Region Manager changes for establishing proper coverage of local marketing areas. Assist in the preparation of Area and District Sales objectives to accomplish the Company's overall objectives.

D. *Distributor Relations Manager–Marketing Division*
Coordinate with the Distributor Relations Manager–Marketing Division on all matters relating to our distributor organization.

E. *Corporate Advertising Manager*
Collaborate with the Corporate Advertising Manager on matters pertaining to advertising, sales promotion, shows and exhibits, local promotion, Company publications and related advertising activities.

F. *Area Sales Managers*
Cooperate with other Area Sales Managers to attain maximum sales, particularly on inter-Area customers and projects.

APPENDIX B—MARKETING MANAGEMENT
JOB DESCRIPTIONS FROM SELECTED COMPANIES

Appendix B—Marketing Management Job Descriptions from Selected Companies

THIS SECTION CONTAINS 29 job descriptions from 23 different companies.

The major marketing functions, such as the head of marketing, marketing managers, sales positions, market research, and advertising heads, are included. Job descriptions for public relations, sales training, sales service, marketing services, and marketing administration managers are also included.

Companies represented include an airplane manufacturer and those dealing in consumer goods, chemicals and pharmaceuticals, oil, and heavy and light industrial equipment.

Although variations exist in job description format, the type of industry makes little difference in the overall structure of the job description.

Most descriptions contain a section devoted to the basic function of the description; a listing of the jobholder's major responsibilities; limits of authority, either described in detail in dollar figures or shown in a broad statement; span of control; and relationships within and outside the organization.

As reported in Chapter 4, the average length of these job descriptions is two pages. Most descriptions included in this section fall into this category, with the exception of the seven-page description for the Director of Marketing at a chemicals company, shown on page 171. In addition to the routine listing of job tasks, this description includes a unique section, "Responsibilities, Relationships, and Limits of Authority of Every Executive," which indicates the basic administrative responsibilities that the company believes are common to all executive jobs. This is one of the few job descriptions submitted that contain a "general" listing of executive duties.

In this section of the study, one may also find both broadly outlined and intricately detailed job descriptions.

Perhaps the most broadly outlined description in this group is that of the Vice President of Marketing for the Union Oil Company, which covers the duties of the top marketing official in less than one page.

On the other hand, the job description for the District Sales Manager at the Koppers Company is divided into 59 major and minor sections. Some of the major headings include descriptions of activities for sales and business development, supervision and administration, sales program and budgets, general duties, authority coverage, and performance measurement criteria.

VICE PRESIDENT OF MARKETING
P. Ballantine & Sons

REPORTS TO: President

SUPERVISES: Vice President of Sales
Merchandising and Promotion Manager
Advertising Manager
Public Relations Manager
Director of Marketing Planning and Research
Market Promotions Manager

BASIC FUNCTION: Responsible for planning, directing, controlling, and coordinating the overall marketing activities of the company to meet or exceed established volume and profit goals within approved budgets.

MAJOR RESPONSIBILITIES

1. Develops for approval by the President long- and short-term marketing objectives and policies concerning
   • Overall sales, advertising, promotion, public relations, and planning and research activities

- Recruitment, training, and development programs for marketing personnel
- Operating budgets to control expenses and allocate efforts for all marketing activities
- Pricing policies to market the company's products profitably and competitively

2. Directs the development of strategic and tactical marketing plans and programs regarding
   - Geographic coverage
   - Product-line composition
   - Price schedules
   - Packaging

3. Approves marketing department organization, manning levels, personnel assignments, and wage and salary programs in accordance with established policies.

4. Reviews and controls the performance of the marketing department by:
   - Evaluating sales performance against quotas
   - Reviewing actual expenses against budgets and established standards
   - Appraising the company's market position relative to that of leading competitors

5. Approves all operating systems and procedures for the collection, analysis, and dissemination of marketing information.

6. Keeps fully abreast of market developments through
   - Personal contact with the trade, distributors, and industry associations
   - Analysis and review of sales, research, and trade reports

7. Represents the company at appropriate industry, trade, and community functions.

PRINCIPAL WORKING RELATIONSHIPS
(Excluding direct reporting and supervisory relationships)

1. Works closely with the general counsel to insure that the marketing activities of the company are conducted in accordance with pertinent statutes and regulations.

2. Works closely with the vice president of finance to provide all data necessary to prepare company reports and financial forecasts.

3. Works closely with the vice president of operations to insure that production and marketing activities are effectively coordinated.

4. Works closely with the director of industrial relations to insure that the personnel activities of the marketing department are in conformance with established companywide personnel policies.

VICE PRESIDENT–MARKETING
Union Oil Company of California

LOCATION: Los Angeles Home Office

Organization

REPORTS TO: Senior Vice President–Refining and Marketing

SUPERVISES: General Manager–Divisional Sales
Manager–Military Sales
Manager–Refinery Bulk Sales
Four Staff Managers (Advertising and Sales Promotion, Merchandising, Real Estate, and Marketing Distribution)

OBJECTIVES

To develop and execute the ———— Refining and Marketing Division's entire marketing program to provide increased sales volume at increasing profitability and appropriate long-range growth.

RESPONSIBILITIES

1. To develop, with his Staff Departments and in accordance with the Company's long-term plan, effective short-range marketing programs to exceed sales goals.
2. To develop input for long-range Company plans in the marketing area.
3. To develop and organize an effective Marketing organization.
4. To maintain close liaison with Executive Management, the Division Planning Department, and other Corporate groups to assist in the shaping of both Company and Marketing Department policies.
5. To establish goals for the Marketing organization.
6. To work closely with line and staff Marketing groups to provide a coordinated approach, within expense budgets, to achieve sales goals and expense budgets.

MANAGER OF MARKETING
The Glidden Company

REPORTS TO: Vice President–General Manager, Pigments and Color Division

[Because of changes in organizational structure at The Glidden Company, the following job description is no longer current. It is included because of its detailed outline of job responsibilities.]

BASIC FUNCTION

Develop practical, innovative marketing policies, plans and programs, carried out by a skilled and efficient organization, to produce profit and market penetration objectives consistent with Group and Company goals.

NATURE AND SCOPE

The incumbent's function deals with a very technical, sophisticated and specialized industrial market. The products marketed are titanium dioxide, its derivatives, inorganic color pigments and lithopone. Under the general guidance of his superior, he manages the total marketing effort, including trade relations, market research, advertising through three geographical sales managers, who have six salesmen assigned. Three product managers, responsible for paint, paper, and rubber and plastics respectively, report to the incumbent. He also controls the technical service function through project assignment, budget preparation and expense approval.

The *Regional Sales Managers* are assigned a defined national area. These managers administer and direct established marketing plans for sales production. No specific account responsibility is assigned the regional sales managers, and market penetration is achieved on a total geographical coverage basis under his direction. House and target accounts are assigned to each manager, by agreement with the incumbent. This manager is expected to evaluate his region's market trends, potential areas of penetration; forecast sales, price and market trends; and import impact. He is charged with operating at minimum costs and approves such expenditures as cars, travel and entertainment, warehouse office facilities, while not given a specific budget. He does not have compensation authority but, conversely, is expected to employ a profit-motivated and effective sales organization and environment. These managers become involved in trade relations only as specified, agreed upon and coordinated by the incumbent.

The *Product Managers* of (*a*) paint, (*b*) paper and allied industries, and (*c*) rubber, plastics and floor tile respectively act in a staff capacity. In each cited area, a manager originates various marketing programs, such as innovative packaging methods, advertising programs, distribution and handling programs subject to incumbent's approval. They deal with customers and the field service organization on product problems and coordinate the technical service program between customers and the development laboratory. Each analyzes product trends and requirements and recommends to his superior required product-line alterations. Approved product-line alterations are then coordinated with the development laboratory. On customer problems a manager may authorize technical service assistance up to $500. A manager has "go or no go" shipping authority on product specifications. He also prepares sales tools, such as brochures, and data sheets, for the field salesmen or customers. The managers also plan the advertising program, budget and objectives, subject to incumbent's approval.

The *Sales Assistant* reports to the incumbent. He maintains and accumulates sales statistics, by customer and market, for purposes of guiding the department's efforts in forecasting, planning and budgeting. The incumbent and the regional and product managers use these data. He also receives sales orders and coordinates them with traffic, including any special instructions, and handles billing accuracy, coding and distribution of invoice copies. He acts as a traffic consultant and obtains freight rates. He maintains mailing lists and product price cards.

The *Sales Manager of Colors*, who is also the Division Manager of St. Helena, acts as a product manager of cadmium color pigments. He provides a technical service function, product complaint-handling function, evaluation of new and present product applicability and trends for the incumbent. He has considerable customer contact and assists in direct selling.

The incumbent is expected to make major industry-company contacts at officer or equivalent level to maintain or solicit sales or discuss trade requirements and relations. The development of industry product specifications or national account specifications or requirements is handled by the incumbent, including the appraisal of existing product lines versus present and future requirements. He negotiates manufacturing representative contracts, assists in credit relations and has final authority on dealings with manufacturing representatives, agents and brokers. Forecasts, budgets, both external and internal publications, advertising, trade relations, technical services, marketing and penetration programs are all subject to incumbent's approval. Prices are established by industry leaders, and ours are adjusted accordingly by the incumbent with the approval of his superior; he develops and determines department's organizational needs and recommends subordinates' compensation. As required, he presents formalized market eoconmic data in relation to production and quality capabilities. He is expected to participate in industry associations, such as NPVL, Sales-Marketing Executives and Chemical Society.

The incumbent operates under the general guidance of the Vice President–General Manager of the Pigments and Color Division and, as such, has considerable latitude of action. Significant, adverse or favorable developments; major changes of effort or direction; budget or expense deviations; and pricing problems are coordinated with his superior.

ACCOUNTABILITIES

1. Effectively maintain top company-industry-customer contacts for maximum market penetration and trade-customer relations.

2. Achieve profit goals and growth consistent with forecasts.
3. Provide innovative and practical marketing, sales, customer services and related objectives and programs in this complex and technical marketing environment.
4. Maintain a profit-motivated sales-service organization highly knowledgeable and able to cope with this technical and sophisticated market.
5. Realistically forecast industry product requirements and originate plans and objectives to continually be competitive with or ahead of market needs.
6. Participate in trade organizations and industrial shows to maintain the corporate image and remain continually aware of industrial product requirements and new fields of market pursuit.

DIRECTOR OF MARKETING
A Chemicals Company

BASIC FUNCTION

Responsible to the General Manager of a Division for management of the Division's total marketing effort and for advice and assistance in the formulation of Division marketing and sales plans. Directs all marketing activities of the Division to achieve planned and approved sales volume and profit objectives and establish the plans, policies, and procedures governing marketing activities of the Division within the general operating plans and policies of the Company and the Division.

GENERAL OBJECTIVES AND RESPONSIBILITIES

Responsibility is assigned and authority granted for the specific duties listed below, as well as those listed under the section of the *Management Guide* entitled "Responsibilities, Relationships, and Limits of Authority of Every Executive." [The section referred to is reprinted following this job description.]

1. Develop sales and profit objectives which relate to customer needs and market opportunities and to plant capacity considerations so that the Company's return on invested capital and its competitive position may be optimized.
2. Supervise the development and execution of comprehensive marketing plans, programs, and budgets through which the Division will meet its sales and profit objectives by meeting customer needs. This respon-

sibility encompasses the full range of marketing strategy formulation and tactical execution, including such areas as pricing, sales methods, and coverage; the nature of sales representation; physical distribution; selection of market segments for special emphasis; promotional and technical support of sales; and specifying the necessary product characteristics, breadth of product line, and means of dealing with captive markets, including forward integration. It necessitates plans in adequate detail as to the means by which sales are to be generated and the source from which they are expected. It calls for allocation of specific responsibility for generating blocs of sales volume among product managers, general line sales, and executive sales activity.

3. Seek assistance of the Vice President–Marketing for sales tasks which are best assigned to members of management outside the Divisional marketing organization.

4. In collaboration with the Controller, supervise the development and application of appropriate measures for monitoring performance against detailed sales and profit objectives and controlling marketing actions to accommodate contingencies revealed by these measures.

5. Direct the regular review of markets and products to identify promising opportunities for creating separate specialty product businesses in areas with distinct product, service, manufacturing, and marketing requirements. Assist in executing the organizational transfer of such businesses into new divisions when decisions for such transfer have been made.

6. Select, evaluate, and develop key executives of the Division marketing organization.

7. Insure that the most effective field sales and distribution organization is maintained to serve market needs.

8. Stimulate demand through development of advertising and promotion programs.

9. Establish standards for product performance and reliability and for field service necessary to compete with maximum effectiveness.

10. Participate directly in selling activities as necessary and at the appropriate level in customer organizations.

11. Provide for a field sales organization to suggest new product and other opportunities for the Company.

12. Make available professional market research, distribution, and other services for other divisions as necessary.

RELATIONSHIP WITH OTHER UNITS IN THE ORGANIZATION

1. Serves as a member of various Company committees as requested.

2. Contacts extradivision personnel as required to arrange for multilevel or top-level sales activities.

3. Works with Research, Development, Corporate Marketing, and other

divisional marketing management on pertinent marketing matters affecting new-product generation or evaluation and coordination of interdivisional marketing activities.

4. Maintains close contact with the Controller in the use of accounting data for control of marketing operations.
5. Collaborates with the Director of Trade Development on matters regarding trade relations interests of the Company.

LIMITS OF AUTHORITY

1. *General*
A. Act in accordance with limits established in the general table, "Limits of Authority," and in the *Appropriation Procedure Manual.*
2. *On Purchase Contracts*
A. Approval of the Division General Manager is required on all commitments exceeding 12 months or where inventory will be raised above 3 months at current rate of disposal.
3. *On Sales Prices*
A. Full authority to apply price schedules determined and approved by the appropriate Division General Manager. Changes in schedule or variations from established schedules of divisional products must be referred to the appropriate Division General Manager.
4. *On Sales Contracts*
A. Nonstandard contracts, including exclusive arrangements with wholesalers, or sales representatives, or special commissions, require the approval of the Division General Manager. Special contracts for divisional products require the approval of the appropriate Division General Manager.
B. Deviations from terms of existing contracts, such as modifying provisions of escalator clauses, require the approval of the Division General Manager for divisional products.
5. *On Operating Methods and Policies*
A. Any major change in distribution, or major changes in wholesale representation, or any geographical changes in the location of sales offices, require the approval of the Division General Manager.

RESPONSIBILITIES, RELATIONSHIPS, AND LIMITS OF AUTHORITY OF EVERY EXECUTIVE
[From *Management Guide*, a Chemicals Company]

Certain basic administrative responsibilities go with every executive job. These responsibilities must be carried out within the framework of overall Company policies, procedures and programs. In this connection, limits have been established on the extent of authority of all executives with respect to certain kinds of actions. Also, appropriate executives have been given functional authority over such activities as legal matters and salaried personnel actions throughout the Company.

To avoid repetition, these common duties, relationships and limits of authority are outlined below. They appear in individual descriptions only where special interpretation or emphasis is required.

Basic Administrative Responsibilities

1. Make long-range plans for the activities under his jurisdiction. To accomplish this he should
   a. Keep informed on any phase of Company plans that will affect the work for which he is responsible.
   b. Establish objectives and detailed plans for the activities under his jurisdiction that will mesh with overall Company plans.
2. Recommend, to the appropriate executives, policies for all activities under his jurisdiction and administer approved Company policies. In this connection he should
   a. Continuously appraise the soundness and adequacy of existing policies.
   b. Receive recommended revisions in Company policies from associates and subordinates.
   c. Recommend appropriate changes to the proper executive.
   d. Interpret Company policies to his subordinates and see that they are understood and carried out.
3. Organize the activities under his jurisdiction. To accomplish this he should
   a. Make certain that all necessary functions are provided.
   b. Assign duties and define the authority of subordinates.
   c. See that all activities are properly coordinated.
   d. Be alert for needs to modify the plan of organization to increase effectiveness or adjust to changing conditions. Receive and give consideration to recommendations from associates and subordinates for revisions and install approved changes.
4. Build and maintain an effective working force or staff to carry out the activities required. In this connection, he should
   a. Select, or approve the selection of, personnel with the proper qualifications to fill subordinate positions for which he is responsible.
   b. Interpret policies and the plan of organization to subordinates, including the latter's own responsibilities.
   c. Train and coach subordinates to do their own work well. Analyze

their strengths and weaknesses and help them to develop themselves accordingly.

d. Develop an understudy for each position, including his own, so that the removal of any individual from the organization would not seriously disrupt operations.

e. Hold conferences and other two-way discussions to keep properly informed on the activities under his jurisdiction and help his subordinates to understand their work in relation to other company activities.

f. Encourage creative effort by maintaining an open mind and constructive attitude toward suggestions and by giving full credit to subordinates for their contributions.

g. Maintain discipline, adjust grievances fairly and promptly and counsel with subordinates to increase morale.

h. Give attention to the interests of employees so as to assure them of proper opportunities for advancement and recognition.

5. See that adequate procedures, methods and techniques are established so that subordinates may do their work with maximum effectiveness and at low cost. In this connection, he should

a. Where appropriate, arrange for the preparation of written guides for the use of personnel.

b. Check compliance with established methods, procedures and techniques.

c. Seek better ways of doing the job. Receive recommendations for changes by associates and subordinates and adopt those which will improve operations.

6. Provide adequate facilities, including working space, equipment, supplies and materials for economical operation. In this connection, it is necessary to

a. Determine the proper location of facilities for optimum operating results and probable expansion.

b. Provide for proper safeguards to persons and properties and for the protection and maintenance of facilities.

7. Direct and coordinate the activities under his jurisdiction. To discharge this responsibility, he should

a. Assign work to subordinates in clear terms.

b. Schedule major operations in sufficient detail so that subordinates can plan their work properly.

c. Supervise operations by personal observation and analysis of records so that work is performed at a minimum cost, with proper standards of quality, quantity and timeliness.

d. Determine that his organization cooperates with and is of maximum assistance to other organizations and the Company.

  e. Clear important matters with his superior and others having functional supervision, whose concurrence is required before action can be taken. Except in emergencies, notify interested parties in advance of contemplated action.

  f. Make decisions promptly in all matters referred by subordinates or associates. He is also responsible for decisions made by subordinates.

8. Assist in the preparation of budgets for the activities under his jurisdiction and control the number of employees and their traveling and other costs and expenses within the budget limits established.

9. Keep his superior fully informed on the progress of activities under his jurisdiction and especially apprise him of new or major developments and important problems encountered.

10. Prepare appropriation requests for expenditures within his jurisdiction and in accordance with provisions set forth in the *Appropriation Procedure Manual.*

RELATIONSHIPS

1. Approval of Chairman, Vice Chairman, or President is required for appointments to executive positions.

2. Functionally responsible to the Director of Employee Relations for cooperation in the clarification and coordination of organization plans and for administration and interpretation of Company personnel policies for salaried and hourly employees under his jurisdiction.

3. Functionally responsible to the Controller for all accounting, statistical, and record-keeping activities of the parent Company and all subsidiaries, wherever located, and for preparation of budgets for activities under his jurisdiction according to approved budgetary control procedures.

4. Functionally responsible to the Secretary and General Counsel for all matters requiring legal interpretation or opinion and for approval of legality of all contracts.

5. Collaborates with the Director of Engineering in the preparation of appropriation requests, conforming to the procedure set forth in the *Appropriation Procedure Manual.*

LIMITS OF AUTHORITY

1. All expenditures of $1,000 and less must be approved by the senior departmental executive. All expenditures exceeding $1,000 must be processed in accordance with the procedure for handling appropriation requests, as set forth in the *Appropriation Procedure Manual.*

2. All matters affecting salaried personnel, including compensation thereof, and the authority of all executives with regard thereto are

established in the section of this *Management Guide* relating to the Employee Policy Committee.

3. All executives may operate within the limits of approved Company policy. New policies, changes in existing policies, and deviations from established policy require approval of the executive next higher in authority.

MANAGER OF MARKET RESEARCH
West Penn Power Company

SUMMARY STATEMENT: Manager of Market Research manages a specialized staff to carry out centralized market research activities in order to determine marketing and economic trends and their effect on our Company's business and to provide staff assistance to general office and field organizations in the area of market research responsibility. Aids the executive in carrying out his reserved responsibilities by assisting him in all phases of the marketing function.

REPORTS TO: Vice President–Marketing

REPORTING TO THE MANAGER OF MARKET RESEARCH: Market Analyst

MAJOR RESPONSIBILITIES

1. Aid the executive in carrying out his reserved responsibilities by conducting investigations, organizing plans and programs, reviewing proposals of staff departments, and making recommendations in all phases of the marketing function.
2. Forecast company size in terms of kilowatt hour sales, revenues, and customers by class of service and by major industrial groups. Forecast net power supply and company peak demands. Develop data, procedures, and techniques to achieve forecasting accuracy.
3. Study, analyze, and interpret national and local economic trends and developments which affect company business and business opportunities.
4. Study markets and applications to determine sales potentials and growth probabilities. Determine saturations, value of applications, and their effect on use of service and revenues.
5. Develop sales control procedures and reporting systems.
6. Assist in establishing sales objectives. Analyze sales performance and

compare divisions. Compare company sales performance with national trends and the experience of other utilities.

7. Plan, conduct, and report on market surveys and studies.
8. Prepare Marketing Group staff operating expense budgets. Analyze and report reasons for deviations. Analyze costs for each marketing section in relation to revenues, customers, and sales accomplishment.

Cooperative Relationships

1. Provide staff assistance in areas of market research responsibility.
2. Advise and assist other department managers on matters relating to market research activities and work with them on matters of mutual concern.
3. Obtain the cooperation of company personnel in carrying out all phases of market research activities.
4. Work with general office staff personnel to develop company policies, plans, programs, and standards affecting the marketing function.
5. Establish and maintain good industry relations by cooperating and working with personnel of other utility companies and electric industry groups.

MANAGER OF MARKETING RESEARCH
Getty Oil Company

BASIC FUNCTION: Collects, interprets, and evaluates internal and external marketing information to assist Division Marketing Management in establishing objectives, selecting alternative courses of action, and appraising and improving the effectiveness of Marketing policies, programs, and performance.

Duties and Responsibilities

1. Advises line Sales Management to ensure that sales efforts are directed toward those geographic markets, product categories, and classes of trade with the greatest volume and profit potentials.
2. Directs the development and implementation of new and established methods for appraising Division sales performance. Recommends action necessary to improve performance based on his analyses.
3. Assists line Sales and Staff Management in developing effective marketing programs by providing and interpreting industry marketing data.
4. Assists the Manager of Advertising in planning and evaluating Division advertising and sales promotion programs.

5. Develops, recommends, supervises, and analyzes consumer and customer surveys of Company product line.
6. Ensures that all Marketing Research studies conducted by outside research agencies are carried out at the lowest possible cost consistent with technical and professional standards.
7. Develops and recommends an annual Marketing Research Program, with related budget estimates.
8. Keeps abreast of industry marketing research methods and activities through contacts with business and trade associations.

PROBLEM SOLVING (GUIDANCE—TYPE)

Under guidance, in accordance with Company policy, and within the framework of accepted practices, determines factors necessary to effectively plan and carry out required marketing programs, selects the best method to secure external information bearing on these factors, and deduces pertinent factual conclusions for use in planning and effectuating the program and, further, devises means of measuring effectiveness of expenditures in carrying out these marketing programs.

ACCOUNTABILITY (FREEDOM TO ACT—IMPACT—MAGNITUDE)

Contributes basic conclusions and data derived from external sources to facilitate planning and evaluation by others of all marketing programs. Broad freedom is granted on choice of techniques and methods in research and experimentation in evaluation of effectiveness measurement.

SUPERVISION RECEIVED (TYPE—DEGREE—TITLE OF SUPERVISOR)

This function falls under the general supervision and guidance of the Manager of Marketing Services.

SUPERVISION EXERCISED (TYPE—DEGREE—TITLES OF POSITIONS SUPERVISED)

Direct supervision of one Marketing Research Analyst and one Statistician. Has functional guidance and responsibility over the employees assigned the tasks of gathering community, customer, and industry information of an intellectual nature and exercises control over outside company employees of marketing research consultants engaged from time to time to provide customer, community, and industry marketing studies.

RECRUITMENT REQUIREMENTS (EDUCATION—EXPERIENCE—SPECIAL SKILLS)

College graduate preferred, with specialty in the area of marketing research and/or operations research. Two to five years' experience in conducting consumer research projects and marketing analysis.

MANAGER–ADVERTISING
Wyandotte Chemicals Corporation

BASIC FUNCTION: Responsible, in accordance with established corporate and divisional policies, practices, and procedures, for the formulation and execution of advertising policy, plans, and programs designed to increase the effectiveness of the marketing effort of the Industrial Chemicals Group.

ORGANIZATIONAL RELATIONSHIP

Accountable to:	Director of Sales
Exerts direct supervision over:	One employee
Type:	Asst. to Manager–Advertising
Approximate number of people for whom responsible:	Three

SPECIFIC RESPONSIBILITIES

1. Formulate and recommend advertising programs for the I.C. Group.
2. Direct and administer the scheduling, planning, and production of approved advertising programs.
3. Direct the activities of the I. C. Group advertising agency in the execution of approved advertising and sales promotion programs.
4. Responsible for the creation, production, and execution of direct-mail programs, literature, and related sales promotion materials and activities in accordance with approved sales objectives and programs.
5. Responsible for making certain that all advertising copy is checked and approved for legal and technical correctness and for compliance with company policy.
6. Responsible for obtaining approval on trade advertising from the Director of Sales and/or respective Marketing Managers. Responsible for obtaining the approval of the Vice President–Operations and/or Director of Sales on all corporate copy.
7. Responsible for maintaining contacts with representatives of advertising media.
8. Responsible for the preparation of the annual advertising budget. Submit budget for approval by Director of Sales and Vice President–Operations.
9. Audit all invoices for advertising costs.
10. Responsible for control of inventories of advertising material.
11. Responsible for the analysis of competitive advertising. Advise Director of Sales and Marketing Managers of new uses, claims, or services for products competitive with I.C. Group products.

12. Responsible for evaluating and reporting effectiveness of individual advertising campaigns, as well as overall advertising program.
13. Responsible for distribution of all advertising material.
14. Responsible for maintaining up-to-date Addressograph mailing records on customers and selected prospects.
15. Prepare and submit annual budget to Director of Sales for controllable departmental operating expenses.
16. Responsible for proper selection of key personnel and for developing the abilities and performance of subordinate personnel by training, counseling, and example.
17. Responsible for the appearance of new or revised product labels, packages, and shipping containers. Obtain approval of Marketing Managers for any change necessary.
18. Responsible for the proper processing of inquiries resulting from advertising efforts.

FUNCTIONAL RELATIONSHIP

1. Collaborate with Marketing Manager and District Field Sales groups, as well as other sales personnel in the formulation of sales and promotional programs.
2. Maintain contacts with salesmen, distributors, and customers to secure suggestions for new ideas relative to advertising and sales promotion activities.
3. Collaborate with Technical Service Department in the preparation of new or revised product labels, packages, and shipping containers.
4. Collaborate, in accordance with company policies, with the Public Relations Department in handling publicity on products, processes, and personnel.
5. Work with, and participate in, industry or professional group conventions or conferences to keep fully informed on general industry trends, sales and promotion methods, and competitive advertising activities; report all matters of interest in these areas to the Director of Sales and to the Marketing Managers of the various divisions.

ADVERTISING MANAGER
The Bemis Company

FUNCTION: The Advertising Manager is responsible to the Vice President and Director of Operations, and is charged with the conduct of the company's advertising and product publicity programs in such a manner as to achieve the most effective and efficient communications with the company's many publics. He is also responsible for the handling of public relations with regard to all phases except financial and will work with the Treasurer on those. While he may delegate some of his responsibility, along with the authority necessary for accomplishment, he may not delegate his accountability.

Responsibility and Authority

Advertising Administration

Prepare and implement the annual advertising budget to achieve maximum profitable sales of Bemis products.

Recommend the media to be used in Bemis advertising, with the goal of achieving optimum coverage with the dollars budgeted.

Initiate and supervise the preparation of advertising, insuring that the message Bemis desires to transmit is presented most effectively.

Supervise the performance of Advertising Department personnel and the maintenance of department files and records.

Prepare programs and arrange for meetings of the Advertising Committee.

See to it that Director of Operations is informed at all times regarding advertising activities.

Present and explain the company advertising program to Bemis sales representatives by appropriate means so that they will be able to make maximum use of the advertising in their sales work.

Sales Promotion

Supervise the editing of the monthly *Bemis Sales Bulletin*.

Supervise the preparation and purchase of such promotional items as book matches, Sight Savers, calendars and Christmas cards and supervise the distribution of these and other promotional items and advertising materials to the sales divisions, assisting the sales divisions to utilize these materials effectively in their sales efforts.

Assist responsible parties in assembling appropriate advertising literature and promotional items for trade expositions so that these expositions can achieve maximum direct and indirect sales. (Usually delegated to the assistant to the advertising manager.)

Publicity and Public Relations

Supervise preparation and release of product publicity articles so as to gain maximum coverage and sales stimulus.

Supervise the preparation and release of publicity releases concerning executive appointments and changes, etc. (This will often encompass supervising the efforts of the public relations firm.)

Assist the public relations firm and company financial and other executives in the preparation and distribution of announcements and releases covering financial or subsidiary activities.

Assist company executives and others in the preparation of speeches and visual aids for various types of meetings, including security analysts.

Assist in or advise on preparation of company movies.

RELATIONSHIPS

Intracompany

Maintain close contact with product directors (or the managers and sales managers of such operations as Tekmold and Visinet Mill) in order to coordinate advertising with the sales programs to achieve maximum sales.

Work with subsidiary companies and, where necessary, those in which we have a joint-venture partner, in order to see that our general policies are followed to the extent possible and that we, through all of these companies, present the desired image to the public.

Preside over the Unified Company Appearance Program (UCAP) to see that our manual is kept up to date and that all concerned are advised in all respects regarding it.

Consult with Market Research Department regarding market data. Consult with General Production Department regarding accuracy of statements made in advertising. Consult with General Personnel Department regarding public relations announcements.

Assist sales divisions with local advertising.

Prepare speech programs with slide presentations and circulars for education of various company units concerning company affairs.

Outside the Company

Maintain constant contact with the company's advertising agency so that the agency's efforts can be closely guided in directions that will insure its maximum contribution to company programs.

Work closely with the company's public relations firm, maintaining a constant flow of information and insuring that the performance is always of high professional caliber.

Represent the general company, where advisable, in outside advertising groups.

PUBLIC RELATIONS MANAGER
P. Ballantine & Sons

FUNCTION AND DESCRIPTION: Responsible for supervising and managing the overall public relations activities of the department and the Company, which are designed to create and maintain favorable acceptance of the Company and its personnel among consumers, local communities, and the general public.

DUTIES

1. Plans and directs appropriate public relations efforts
   a. To create favorable company identification among consumers and the general public.
   b. To support and complement Company marketing programs.
   c. To publicize operational activities of the Company in business and local communities.
2. Supervises, manages, and controls assigned public relations activities, including:
   a. Promotion of relations with radio and television networks, periodical and newspaper publishers, and other related organizations.
   b. Promotion of relations with community associations, civic leaders, social or fraternal clubs, and commercial associations affiliated with local communities.
   c. Establishment and operation of appropriate public relations services, such as: a film library, photographic services, speakers' bureau, guided plant tours.
   d. Preparation and publishing of 3-Ring newspaper.
3. Arranges for appropriate outside services by public relations firms, subject to final management approval.

4. Insures that public relations efforts are being provided and executed in all designated marketing areas.
5. Coordinates his division's activities with those of other company and department units to take advantage of or create appropriate public relations opportunities.

WORKING RELATIONSHIPS

1. Reports to the Vice President of Marketing.
2. Supervises Public Relations staff and supportive clerical personnel.
3. Works closely with marketing staff managers to create and follow up on appropriate public relations opportunities.
4. Works closely with departments other than marketing in providing and creating favorable public relations services.

VICE PRESIDENT–MERCHANDISING
Indian Head Inc.

BASIC FUNCTION: The basic function of the Vice President–Merchandising is to develop and direct the execution of comprehensive merchandising policies, strategies and programs for product lines, with the objective of maximizing profits and return on investment.

WORKING RELATIONSHIPS

REPORTS TO: Vice President and General Manager

RESPONSIBILITIES AND AUTHORITY

Within the limits of established corporate and division policies and budgets, he is responsible for and has authority to
1. Establish short- and long-range merchandising objectives with respect to both existing and planned styles.
2. Supervise and approve the establishment of product-line styles, specific product-line prices, product identity, put-up, F.O.B. point, quality standards. Insure that adequate quality controls are maintained. Constantly review the styles in terms of current and future market requirements and approve the modification of existing styles or the introduction of new styles.
3. Constantly review activities of the Merchandising Departments, to the end that they are being operated efficiently and within budget.

4. Support sales organization by insuring that the Merchandising Departments give Sales the necessary facts and guidance as to general product information, availability, etc. Work with Sales Managers by visiting key customers, seeking recommendations from the Sales Force and gathering customer playbacks.

5. Establish maximum and minimum inventory levels and supervise the maintenance thereof.

6. Maintain control over greige goods procurement:
    a. Establish guidelines as to pricing and quantities.
    b. Approve selection of greige and finishing sources.
    c. Maintain personal contact with key sources.

7. Provide Controller with necessary data for budget preparations and revisions. Take appropriate action on variations from budget as reported to him by Controller.

8. Make recommendations and suggestions to division management regarding the promotion and advertising of fabrics converted by departments under his supervision. Cooperate with the Advertising Department and Sales Managers in working out and seeking promotional help from fiber companies. Initiate fiber company contact in all cases involving new fabrics.

9. Direct the application of personnel policies and procedures in his departments relating to employment, training, compensation and employee relations.

10. Supervise all warehousing activities.

11. Constantly review activities of Plant Manager to the end that his operation is being operated efficiently and within budget.

12. Make recommendations in any area of division operations which will enhance profits and return on investment.

PRODUCT MANAGER
Koppers Company Inc.

UNIT: Tar & Chemical Division

RESPONSIBLE TO: Sales Manager

BROAD SCOPE OF ACTIVITY

1. To acquire and maintain a high degree of knowledge of the markets and industries in which assigned products are sold.

2. Supervision and coordination of commercial sales activities of assigned products as a staff function.

Specific Responsibility and Authority

I. *Sales and Business Development*

To acquire and develop an understanding of, and be familiar with, specific markets and industries which could become major users of assigned products.

A. To develop, recommend and coordinate marketing programs leading to the expansion of profitable sales volume of assigned products.

B. To innovate ways to expand Koppers' business opportunities through development of new markets or uses for assigned products and through the addition of new products to satisfy customers' needs.

C. To make sales calls with Sales Representatives and/or Districts Sales Managers to get firsthand information on trends and conditions in the market and/or industry and to aid the Districts in their sales efforts.

D. To attend sales conferences, association meetings, conventions to promote sales of Koppers' products and services.

II. *Planning*

A. To originate, develop and recommend marketing programs and techniques designed to give Koppers a position of stature and leadership within the industry and/or market for assigned products.

B. To develop and recommend sales objectives for assigned products within specific markets or industries, including sales volume and profit forecasts.

C. To develop and recommend plans and programs to achieve assigned goals.

III. *Supervision and Administration*

A. *Supervision*

1. To assist the Sales Manager in the training of Sales Representatives; this involves
    a. Selling techniques.
    b. Uses of assigned products.
    c. Competitive situations likely to be encountered.
    d. General market picture of assigned products.
2. To coordinate and facilitate the exchange of information

between sales districts, Product Development Department and between units of the Sales Department.

3. To coordinate activities of the districts for assigned products, involving

    a. Sales coverage.

    b. Customer relations.

    c. Customer complaints.

    d. Product performance information.

    e. Improvement of Sales Representatives' effectiveness.

B. *Administration*

1. To recommend merchandising policies for assigned products within specific markets and/or industries, such as

    a. Sales prices.

    b. Terms of sales.

    c. Discounts.

2. To continually study the potential and actual demands for assigned products and their profitability. To recommend to the Sales Manager

    a. Products which should be dropped.

    b. Improvements to present products which are required to expand present markets.

    c. New products which can be profitably integrated with the present line.

    d. Levels of inventories to be maintained to assure proper customer service.

3. To analyze the activities of competition on assigned products and keep management informed on the following:

    a. New competitors.

    b. New competing products.

    c. New merchandising policies.

    d. New prices.

    e. New sales promotion programs.

4. To prepare special studies and reports in connection with assigned products, as may be requested by the Sales Manager.

IV. *Programs and Budgets*

A. To collaborate with the Sales Manager in the preparation of three-month sales estimates and the annual and three-year sales programs for assigned products.

B. To review sales, by industry and customer, for the purpose of determining progress toward sales goals for assigned products.

V.   *General*

    A.   To assist the Manager, Advertising and Sales Promotion, in the selection, planning and evaluation of advertising and sales promotion programs.

    B.   To collaborate with the Manager, Advertising and Sales Promotion, in the preparation of technical sales literature.

    C.   To coordinate his activities for assigned products and cooperate with other Koppers Divisions or Departments in matters of mutual concern.

VI.   *Authority*

    A.   To operate within the limits of authorized policies, pricing schedules and procedures.

MEASUREMENT OF PERFORMANCE

I.   The measures of performance of this position are

    A.   The strengthening of Koppers' position in the specific markets and industries.

    B.   Volume of profitable sales and its relation to quota and programs for assigned products.

    C.   The soundness of policies and procedures recommended to the Sales Manager.

    D.   The initiative and imagination reflected in ideas for new sales and business opportunities.

    E.   The cordiality of relations which exist between the Product Manager and other units, both within and outside the Corporation.

GROUP BRAND MANAGER
A Food Products Company

BASIC RESPONSIBILITIES

Under the general direction of the Director of Marketing, is responsible for providing overall guidance, coordination, and direction in the marketing of all products in his assigned product group to achieve stated profit and marketing objectives within the framework of Division and Company policies, budgets, and long-range plans.

Specific Duties

1. Develops and recommends to Director of Marketing overall objectives and strategies, both near- and long-term, for the marketing of his assigned product group, in support of objectives and strategies of the Division.

2. Reviews and counsels Brand Managers in the development of volume, share-of-market, and profit objectives for their assigned products, together with complete marketing plans and programs for the achievement of those objectives; ensures coordination of plans and programs within and beyond his assigned product group.

3. Oversees the development of the most profitable line of products within his assigned product group, through planned introduction of new varieties and regular review and suspension of unprofitable varieties.

4. Collaborating with the Director of Marketing Research, develops and maintains a continuous program of research and analysis to obtain information essential to the effective marketing of products in his assigned group.

5. Oversees and counsels with his Brand Managers in the development of sales and share-of-market forecasts for products in his assigned group, together with the analysis of sales and product performance reports.

6. Oversees and counsels with the Brand Managers in establishing and maintaining continuous programs of coordinated commercial research for their assigned products to develop and interpret factual information regarding consumer needs and preferences, competitive conditions, market position, and industry trends and trade practices.

7. Oversees and counsels with Brand Managers in developing advertising plans and programs for their assigned products, in line with approved advertising policies and budgets and in coordination with advertising plans and programs of other products and product groups.

8. Oversees and counsels with Brand Managers in the development of coordinated merchandising and promotion plans, schedules, circulars, and materials for their assigned products.

9. Oversees and counsels with Brand Managers in their development of advertising, merchandising, and other expense budgets for products and activities under his direction, presenting consolidated budget recommendations for management approval.

10. Ensures proper planning, scheduling, and coordination in the development, testing, and market introduction of new and improved varieties and packs for his assigned product group.

11. Oversees and counsels with Brand Managers as they maintain prices, terms, and discounts for products in his assigned group at competitive, profitable levels; recommends changes in line with Company policies, sales, and profit objectives and applicable laws and regulations.

12. Keeps continuously informed of industry and trade developments, makes periodic field sales and factory visits. Analyzes trends and recommends changes, as appropriate, in production and distribution arrangements for his assigned product group; participates in professional, industry, and trade association meetings and other activities.

13. Keeps continuously alert to ideas for new varieties, new products, and other new developments that are potentially applicable to business, referring such ideas through appropriate channels to the New Products Department for evaluation and development, if merited.

14. Presents overall marketing strategy recommendations for his assigned product group at the Annual Strategy Meeting, introducing Brand Managers for individual product strategy presentations.

15. Selects, appoints, trains, periodically counsels, evaluates, and recommends changes in personnel status of Brand Managers and other employees assigned to his direction.

16. Maintains contact with key General Office and field sales personnel and with important customers to follow up on marketing programs and to keep informed on needs of the sales force and on marketing conditions throughout the country.

17. Periodically reviews customer and consumer complaints and suggestions concerning products in assigned group and oversees Brand Managers response and follow-up.

VICE PRESIDENT, SALES
A Chemicals Company

GENERAL STATEMENT OF DUTIES: Responsible for the efficient operation and coordination of all Field Sales Operations of the Division. Responsible for meeting assigned sales objectives and obtaining a major share of the markets for the Division's products in a manner consistent with the Divisional Objectives. Responsible for branch warehousing and distribution to domestic trade channels and developing and maintaining desirable contacts with trade groups.

Duties and Responsibilities

1. *Reports to:* Executive Vice President

2. *Marketing Objectives*
   Participates in the formulation of marketing objectives, policies, plans, and programs. Administers those that are approved for sales operations.

Regularly coordinates, reviews, evaluates, and reports results, including recommendations for changes. Assures that all members of his staff are thoroughly familiar with the approved objectives, policies, plans, and programs.

3. *Plans and Programs*

Directs the preparation of, and approves or obtains approval for, plans and programs for field sales and distribution to meet the long- and short-range sales objectives of the Division and regularly evaluates and reports on results.

4. *Personnel*

Develops and maintains a sales organization capable of coordinated, imaginative, and vigorous selling of the Division's products for the effective achievement of Divisional objectives. Generally directs the recruitment, selection, development, and deployment of effective field personnel, including training for product knowledge, detailing techniques and familiarization with objectives, policies, plans, and programs. Strives to improve quality of all personnel and provides ample opportunity for development at all levels. Reports on the adequacy of compensation plans.

5. *Distribution*

Responsible for recommending an efficient distribution system for the Division's short- and long-term objectives. Establishes and directs the approved system.

6. *Trade Relations*

Generally directs the establishment and maintenance of those contacts and programs necessary for the maintenance of sound business relations with trade groups of interest to the Division. Regularly reports to the Executive Vice President on important trade, professional, and business conditions encountered in the field.

7. *Pricing*

Participates in the formulation of pricing policies and proposals. Regularly reviews and reports to the Executive Vice President on the effect of our pricing, as reported by our field sales and branch personnel. Recommends changes, where desirable, to achieve Division and Company objectives.

8. *Controls and Standards of Measurement*

Directs the use of established controls and standards of measurement and regularly evaluates and recommends changes as required. Takes or recommends corrective action as required.

9. *Profit Planning*

Directs the preparation of the profit plans for his area of responsibility, secures approval, and subsequently develops regional profit plans within the framework of established Divisional plans for gross sales, returned goods, and allowances. In addition, has responsibility for preparing more specific plans for increasing the Division's share of Government business. Regularly evaluates results and takes or recommends corrective action as required.

MEASUREMENT OF PERFORMANCE

1. Attaining or exceeding assigned profit plan objective.
2. Adherence and conformance to Division plans and programs.
3. Maintenance of excellent two-way communication between field and branch personnel and the home office.

VICE PRESIDENT, SALES MANAGER
P. Ballantine & Sons

FUNCTION AND DESCRIPTION:

Responsible for directing all sales and sales service activities to meet or exceed approved volume and revenue goals.

DUTIES:

1. Develops and recommends sales volume goals, revenue objectives, and expense budgets by geographic areas, product categories, and channels of distribution.
2. Recommends year-ahead sales program, which includes
   a. Product line and sales channel emphasis.
   b. Product and package promotion plans.
   c. Sales quotas and operating budgets.
3. Directs and controls all sales and sales service activities to achieve or exceed approved sales volume and revenue objectives.
4. Recommends the organization structure appropriate to achieve the desired sales volume.
5. Participates in the selection, training, evaluation, promotion, and dismissal of the executives reporting directly to him.
6. Recommends compensation levels and incentive plans for sales employees.

7. Recommends the most effective distribution pattern for the Company's products.
8. Recommends and administers Company policies for the selection and evaluation of distributors.
9. Keeps abreast of significant industry trends and development through
   a. Personal visits with sales personnel and key retail and distributor accounts.
   b. Review of market activity reports from sales and market research field personnel.
   c. Participation in appropriate industry and trade organizations and activities.

WORKING RELATIONSHIPS:

1. Reports to the Vice President of Marketing.
2. Supervises various division sales managers.
3. Works closely with the managers of advertising, merchandising, and promotion and public relations to coordinate their activities with those of headquarters and field sales personnel.
4. Works closely with the director of marketing planning and research to provide free interchange of mutually beneficial information.

SALES MANAGER
Schering Corporation

REPORTS TO: Vice President, Schering Laboratories

FUNCTION: To manage and plan the field staff activities in support of domestic products and sales policies. Administer Government/Hospital Sales, Sales Services, Sales Training, and Sales Administration.

SCOPE OF RESPONSIBILITIES

- Participate with Rx and O.T.C. Marketing Managers in the preparation of marketing plans, budgets, and schedules as preliminarily approved by the Vice President for Marketing.
- In conjunction with the Advertising Manager, assist in the planning and timing of promotional efforts and on the relative emphasis to be placed on personal versus impersonal selling.
- Participate with O.T.C. and Rx Marketing in the planning of the field

sales program and relative emphasis required for trade and professional selling.

- Direct the organization of field selling activity, the number and type of representatives to be employed, their distribution geographically, and their assignments by market segments (hospital, Government, industrial, professional, trade, etc.).
- Set standards of field selling and supervisory performance and check actual operations against standards.
- Recommend methods of compensation and other conditions of employment, including incentive systems.
- Direct the sales training program.
- Review and approve all general communications between home office marketing personnel and the field organization.
- Cooperate closely with marketing product managers, contributing information on field marketing conditions, prices, competition, new product forms, unfilled needs, criticisms of Schering products, etc. Receive current information on marketing plans, including schedules, budgets, product changes, etc.
- Advise the Medical Services Director of supporting activity needed from that department for field operations.
- Supply information to the Vice President for Marketing, Vice President, O.T.C. and Distribution, and Product Managers on factors influencing the success or failure of programs as executed in the field.

SUPERVISES

Directly   (8)   4 Regional Managers, Sales Services Manager, Sales Training Manager, Government and Hospital Sales Manager, Sales Analysis Manager.

Indirectly (444) Sales Communications Manager, Field Sales Operations Manager, Assistant Sales Training Manager, Assistant Government and Hospital Sales Manager, 34 Division Managers, approximately 405 representatives.

RELATIONSHIPS

Within the Company

Advise the Vice President, Schering Laboratories, Vice President, O.T.C. and Distribution, and the Marketing Managers regarding the sales implementation of proposed marketing plans.

Advise the Medical Services Director regarding supportive activity from that department relative to the field staff effort.

Participate in the formulation of decisions relating to marketing objectives and policies and marketing programs.

Outside the Company

Attend various professional and trade association meetings.

Call on various distribution outlets (wholesalers, large chain distributors, etc.) as required.

POSITION REQUIREMENTS

Bachelor's degree, plus 12–15 years of related marketing experience, with thorough knowledge of pharmaceutical industry, distribution, and trade. Broad knowledge of sales and merchandising techniques. Knowledge of personnel and management techniques.

GENERAL SALES MANAGER
Bobbie Brooks, Inc.

BASIC FUNCTION: The General Sales Manager directs the activities of the field sales personnel in achieving sales quotas and accomplishing the objectives of the company's sales programs. Stimulates the sales force and develops enthusiasm for selling the entire line.

REPORTS TO:

Vice President, Marketing

SUPERVISES:

New York Regional Sales Manager
Cleveland Regional Sales Manager
Chicago Regional Sales Manager
Atlanta Regional Sales Manager
Dallas Regional Sales Manager
Los Angeles Regional Sales Manager
Assistant to the General Sales Manager

MAJOR DUTIES AND RESPONSIBILITIES

1. Proposes programs for promoting the sale of all the company's lines.
2. Devises selling methods and techniques to be employed by the outside sales force.

3. Recommends the type and size of the sales force required to serve the sales territories and the Bobbie Brooks accounts.
4. Recommends the territorial boundaries and the sales quotas to be met by territories and in total.
5. Selects, terminates, as well as appraises the productivity of, the field sales personnel.
6. Advises on the compensation arrangement for field sales personnel.
7. Recommends the expenditure items and the amounts to be provided in the operating budget for the field sales activity.
8. Works with salesmen in the field through the Regional Managers to give training in selling methods, to provide assistance in developing customer contacts and sales territories and to generally improve customer relations.
9. Assign sales personnel to territories and accounts in the manner that will make the best use of sales talent and provide the best service to customers.
10. Coordinates with customer service department to assure that customer inquiries are properly channeled for handling to the department responsible.
11. Coordinates with the individual Merchandising Managers to see that each apparel line receives its fair share of attention.
12. Insures that salesmen are provided with needed assistance or service, such as delivery information for each group or item in the line, swatch books, reproduction of advertisements, photographs, and the like.
13. Reviews reports of progress and conditions from the Regional Managers, giving credit for good performance and taking remedial steps as the case requires.
14. Reviews the line with Merchandising at several steps of completion to be able to plan a sales strategy in line with the overall merchandising plans.
15. Counsels with the Director of Merchandising and individual Merchandising Managers at frequent intervals to provide the field reactions to current and proposed styles.
16. Works closely with the Regional Managers to keep in touch with the ease or difficulty of selling each part of the line and to keep informed on how the goods are moving out of customers' stores.
17. Assists in showing of the line to salesmen and Regional Managers at the line-release meetings.
18. Works with the Regional Managers on use of sales statistics and other sales and marketing data to assure that maximum benefit is derived from the provided information.
19. Counsels with the Assistant to the Vice President, Marketing, to determine the need for additional or revised sales data.

20. Cooperates with the Sales Training Manager to upgrade the caliber and productivity of the sales force.
21. Reviews and approves Regional Manager expense accounts and sales expenditures.
22. Makes personal calls on large-volume customers and prospective customers as required.
23. Reviews and approves overall and individual region sales quotas.
24. Appraises sales coverage against statistics, sales results against quotas and sales costs against budgets; directs the activities of the salesmen to obtain improved performance.

DIRECTOR OF SALES
Controls Company of America

PRIMARY FUNCTION AND RESPONSIBILITY

Directs the field sales efforts to attain the Division's objectives.

RELATIONSHIPS

Line: Reports TO: Vice President and General Manager
Supervises: Product Line Managers, Regional Sales Manager, Industrial and Commercial Controls Manager, Supervisor, Marketing Services, Sales Engineers

TYPICAL DUTIES AND RESPONSIBILITIES

1. Develops a sound organization by properly staffing, training and guiding suitable personnel to perform the necessary functions effectively and economically.
2. Reviews periodically the performance and salaries of subordinates and recommends necessary adjustments in conformance with Company policies and procedures.
3. Administers the department within the budget limitations and in accordance with policies and procedures of the Company and Division.
4. Plans, directs and coordinates the activities of the department and staff to assure the achievement of departmental objectives.
5. Builds an alert, well-trained sales force and utilizes its efforts effectively and economically.
6. Develops and recommends a suitable sales program to attain the desired market penetration.

7. Encourages a high level of service to the customer, utilizing recognized and established practices within Division and Company policies.
8. Proposes the general quality standards that are acceptable to the market for a specific product.
9. Assists in preparing periodic forecasts of customers' requirements by product.
10. Keeps informed of product developments, policy changes and product activities of all major competition.
11. Executes the approved sales programs.
12. Encourages department personnel to transmit ideas for new products and the improvement of existing products.
13. Maintains favorable relationships with the management of customers and prospective customers.
14. Assures that sales personnel have available pertinent sales aids.
15. Recommends the applicable price level that will maintain existing markets and develop new ones.
16. Establishes and maintains channels for the flow of customer information from the field to sales administration.
17. Determines suitable territories and measures performance.
18. Plans periodic sales meetings.
19. Plans meetings for the explanation of new products.
20. Supports the sales effort in parallel to the direct approach by planning executive contacts with the several echelons of customer personnel.
21. Submits to the Vice President and General Manager for his approval
    a. Product group sales forecast.
    b. Product group budget.
    c. Expense budget.
22. Delegates responsibilities to his subordinates, with corresponding authority; directs them in their functions; and establishes suitable standards and controls so that department performance can be measured and reported.
23. As a member of the Division Staff, advises the Vice President and General Manager in establishing Division objectives, in developing Division policies and in implementing Division procedures.
24. Advises in the development of a product line, recommending additions and deletions as market conditions dictate.
25. Collaborates with all other departments in the attainment of Company objectives.
26. Represents the Division on special assignments, as directed.
27. Stays abreast of the latest developments and techniques in the industry and constantly appraises their adaptability to Company operation.
28. Keeps the Vice President and General Manager informed of all pertinent matters.

29. Represents the Company at professional and industrial activities as directed, conducting himself at all times in a manner that is a credit to himself and the Company.

DISTRICT SALES MANAGER
Koppers Company Inc.

RESPONSIBLE TO: Sales Manager

BROAD SCOPE OF ACTIVITY:

1. Responsible for attaining maximum profitable sales volume through the effective direction and supervision of the district sales organization.
2. To maintain the most profitable cost-to-sales ratio.

SPECIFIC RESPONSIBILITIES AND AUTHORITY

I. *Sales and Business Development*

    A. To develop, promote, and secure maximum profitable sales of assigned products in the designated market area of responsibility.
        1. Work through and with Sales Representatives to maintain a close relationship with *major* customers
            a. To obtain maximum profitable sales volume of assigned products.
            b. To understand customers' needs and potential product requirements.
            c. To consult with customers on their product problems and complaints.
            d. To be sure that customers recognize the District Manager's and Koppers' personal interest in them.
    B. To innovate ways, and keep abreast of opportunities, to expand the business fields of Koppers through development of new markets.
        1. To search for new uses for existing products.
        2. To search for new ideas for new products.
        3. To identify opportunities for the addition of new products through
            a. Development.
            b. Acquisition.
        4. To contact proper Company personnel when customers in-

dicate needs which could be satisfied by products or services of other Koppers departments or divisions. To coordinate such contacts with customers through appropriate Koppers channels.

C.   To attend sales conferences, association meetings, and conventions to promote sales of Koppers products and services.

II. *Supervision and Administration*

A.   To supervise and coordinate the work of the sales force and office personnel of the assigned district.

   1.   Sales Representatives.

      a. To direct and assist Sales Representatives to

         1. Accomplish sales quotas and overall sales objectives.

         2. Prepare annual sales program.

         3. Control and reduce selling expense.

         4. Furnish necessary reports and information as requested.

      b. Training.

         1. To provide coaching on

            a. Sales techniques.

            b. Use of selling tools.

            c. Application of policies.

            d. Product education.

         2. To assist on field contacts, as required.

         3. To furnish counsel on difficult problems.

   2.   Office Personnel.

      a. To direct and assist office personnel to

         1. Coordinate and report district activities accurately and promptly.

         2. Cooperate with main office, plants, and other Company departments.

         3. Assist Sales Representatives as required.

         4. Handle customers' telephone calls and correspondence promptly and courteously.

B.   Administration.

   1.   To approve travel expenses, purchase requisitions, etc.

   2.   To work with existing district office personnel through established channels to make certain that orders are properly handled and customers' needs are serviced.

   3.   To review the performance of each individual approximately on an annual basis and discuss such rating personally with the employee.

   4.   To submit recommendations for salary increases for his personnel when performance merits such action.

    5. To submit to the Sales Manager monthly activity reports setting forth results obtained on major activities, significant trends, and unusual occurrences, such as

      a. Product acceptance.

      b. Quality and uniformity of assigned products.

      c. Market trends.

      d. Competitive situation.

      e. Prices.

      f. Problems.

III.   *Sales Programs and Budgets*

    A. To develop and submit annual sales volume objectives and to prepare and recommend an annual budget for sales force and district office expense.

    B. To be responsible for meeting approved sales and budget programs and for maintaining most profitable cost-to-sales ratios.

IV.   *General*

    A. To place into operation sales plans and activities developed by Company management.

    B. To make recommendations to the Sales Manager for more efficient organization in line with sales objectives.

    C. To create and recommend new and better selling techniques and methods.

    D. To maintain working relationships with other district managers of his own, as well as all Divisions, to further Company sales.

    E. To coordinate communication between the home office and customers on policy and technical matters.

    F. To establish and maintain good relationships with customers, industry, and community.

V.   *Authority*

    A. To operate within the limits of authorized policies, pricing schedules, and procedures.

MEASUREMENT OF PERFORMANCE

I.   *The measures of performance of this position are*

    A. Volume of profitable district sales and its relation to quota and programs.

    B. The maintenance of a profitable cost-to-sales ratio.

C. The initiative and imagination reflected in ideas for new sales and business opportunities.

D. The example of good management, high morale, personal conduct, and effective teamwork evidenced by the District Manager and his staff in their contacts with members of the Corporation and others.

E. The general goodwill and product acceptance created and maintained in the district.

DISTRICT SALES MANAGER
A Brewery

IMMEDIATE SUPERVISOR: Region Sales Manager

RESPONSIBILITY: In a line capacity is responsible for the successful execution of the Sales Program and for the sale and consumer acceptance of the product within his district.

DUTIES

In connection with this responsibility, the principal duties are

1. To assist in the planning of the Sales Program and to effectively execute this program within his district.
2. To assist in the selection of additional sales personnel for his area.
3. To supervise and continually train sales personnel under his jurisdiction.
4. To evaluate the performance of distributors in his district and to recommend to the Region Sales Manager and home office cancellations and appointments of distributors.
5. To control sales expense in his area.
6. To supervise distribution and erection of advertising material.
7. To inform the Division Sales Manager and Region Manager, on a continuing basis, as to the current competitive and general sales conditions in his district.
8. To plan and conduct sales meetings in his district.

AUTHORITY

1. To conduct a sales program within his district.
2. To assist in the selection of additional sales personnel for his district.

3. To supervise and train sales personnel under his jurisdiction.
4. To evaluate and make recommendations regarding distributors within his district.
5. To control sales expense in his district.
6. To supervise the distribution and erection of advertising material.
7. To plan and conduct sales meetings in his district.

REGIONAL SALES MANAGER
Bobbie Brooks, Inc.

BASIC FUNCTION: The Regional Sales Manager is the field sales executive responsible for the sale of all of the Company's lines in a specified sales region. He reports to the General Sales Manager and is directly responsible for achieving sales objectives in his region. He directs the efforts of all salesmen in his region to assure budgeted performance.

REPORTS TO: General Sales Manager

SUPERVISES: Territory Salesmen and Office Staff

MAJOR DUTIES AND RESPONSIBILITIES

1. Develops marketing plans and programs for his region for submission to the General Sales Manager for approval.
2. Recommends, to the General Sales Manager, specific territorial assignments for the salesmen.
3. With the help of each salesman, develops a sales forecast and from it develops the overall regional sales forecasts and budgets and submits them to the Field Sales Manager for incorporation in the overall marketing forecasts and budgets.
4. Works with each salesman to develop a plan to be followed in working his territory. This plan should include a list of key potential accounts to be developed, as well as a pattern for covering his territory.
5. Appraises the performance of each salesman on a continuing basis and offers specific suggestions for improvement in salesman's performance.
6. Sees that each salesman is fully equipped with the sample line, swatch books and other sales aids before setting out to sell each line.
7. Periodically checks the salesmen's sample lines to be sure that all current garments are being carried and that all recalled items have been taken out of the sample line.

8. Makes sales calls with individual salesmen to demonstrate how to sell the company's products.
9. Personally works with the sales trainees in his region to assure that they are getting maximum training during their period of employment in his region.
10. Holds periodic sales meetings to disseminate information and to train the territory salesmen.
11. Stimulates the salesmen to submit ideas and success stories or new techniques on how to sell the company's lines and sees that this information is disseminated throughout the sales force.
12. Handles major accounts on a personal basis as assigned by the General Sales Manager.
13. Keeps the General Sales Manager fully informed of progress and any significant developments in the region.
14. Reviews sales performance reports and takes the necessary action to correct unsatisfactory results.

GENERAL SALES MANAGER–EASTERN REGION
International Milling Company

OBJECTIVE: To direct all bakery flour and bakery mix sales activities and related staff functions in the Eastern Region. To maximize the long-term profitability of the region through an optimum combination of sales volumes, conversions, and cost control. The Eastern Region includes the seaboard area from the District of Columbia through New England, New York, Pennsylvania, and New Jersey. The region accounts for about _____ percent of the Company's bakery flour sales.

RELATIONSHIPS

Reports on line basis to: Division Vice President and General Sales Manager–Bakery Products.

Supervises on a line basis: Assistant General Sales Manager, Bakery Flour Sales Manager, Bakery Mix Sales Manager, District Sales Manager–Sales Office Manager, and Credit Manager. Indirectly supervises approximately 30 other sales and administrative sales personnel and 25 employees in the various staff sections.

SPECIFIC RESPONSIBILITIES

1. Maximize profitability of bakery flour sales in the Eastern Region. Plan sales objectives and programs. Direct the Bakery Flour Sales

Manager in the implementation of the programs and achievement of objectives.

2. Maximize profitability of bakery mix sales in the Eastern Region. Direct activities of the Bakery Mix Sales Manager in providing training, promotion, and technical and sales assistance to the bakery flour salesmen who are also responsible for the sale of bakery mix products. Ensure effective coordination between bakery mix and bakery flour activities and with the activities of the Minneapolis and Lockport bakery mix departments.

3. Control expenses of the Eastern Region. Maintain sales, administrative, delivery, and warehouse costs at a level giving overall optimum return. Prepare periodic profit and expense projections for the General Sales Manager–Bakery Products and be accountable for these projections.

4. Control the extension of credit. Review all credit limits and credit practices recommended by the Credit Manager and revise as necessary. Ensure that all credit policies are effectively implemented, that credit practices are consistent with sales requirements, and that limits are consistent with the customer's financial status.

5. Ensure that all staff and administrative sales activities are performed effectively and to the maximum benefit of the sales organization. Includes accounting, production scheduling, credit, office services, and activities of Sales Correspondents. Ensure that New York office personnel coordinate effectively with other IMCo locations and departments as required.

6. Develop an effective sales force and administrative organization. Plan and initiate changes in organization structure; select key subordinates; and provide appropriate direction, control, and opportunities for advancement and development. Ensure the development of an effective training program within the region for all job categories.

7. Develop and project budget for all areas of the region.

8. Control pricing of all products within limits set by General Sales Manager-Bakery Products (GSM). Assist GSM in determining national sales policy. Ensure that any delegated pricing activity is properly applied.

9. Personally sell and service certain major accounts. Develop and maintain sales volume and obtain maximum conversions consistent with long-term profit and sales considerations. Responsible for handling of Quality Bakers of America accounts and sells or contributes heavily to sales credited to other Company locations.

10. Develop and maintain current knowledge of factors affecting long- and short-run sales and profit outlook. Includes such factors as customer requirements and financial status, general economic conditions, weather and crop conditions, Government programs, transportation costs, and consumption trends.

ACCOUNTABILITY FACTORS

Eastern Region flour sales are about _____ hundredweight annually. Bakery mix sales are about _____ hundredweight annually; total sales, $_____. Annual budget is about $_____.

POSITION SPECIFICATIONS

Education—College degree or equivalent in work experience. Position requires continued education in management, marketing, and technical subjects.

Experience—15 years' company experience, including 5 years' heavy sales experience, 5 years' sales management, and 2 years in some combination of production, traffic, or production scheduling.

Other qualifications—Superior management and sales ability; complete knowledge of Company products and of transit theory and practice; good understanding of production methods, grain buying and costing, laboratory functions, and advertising; and working knowledge of baking.

DIVISION SALES MANAGER
Union Oil Company of California

PRINCIPAL JOB RESPONSIBILITIES AND DUTIES

MK-20

LOCATION: Division Office

ORGANIZATION

Reports to: General Manager–Divisional Sales

Supervises: Sales Manager–Commercial (1 or 2)
Sales Manager–Retail (2 to 4)
Sales Manager–Area (1 or 2) Not found in all Divisions
Manager of Personnel & Training
Real Estate Representative (2 to 5)
Manager–Services & Operations
Supervisor of Accessory Sales
Merchandiser (1 or 2)
Real Estate Supervisor (3 Divisions only)

OBJECTIVES

To direct and coordinate the activities of the Division in achieving the maximum profitable volume of both retail and commercial sales. To minimize administrative staff and delivery expense without the loss of service to the field.

RESPONSIBILITIES

1. To formulate and execute Division and Companywide sales programs that will continuously improve the position of Union Oil.
2. To direct the development of goals and expense budgets for all Division levels and submit them for review and approval; to transmit approved goals and expense budgets to the Division organization as standards for performance.
3. To direct Divisional sales and service activities to attain those goals.
4. To make pricing decisions within delegated authority to optimize profit and sales level of the Division.
5. To achieve and maintain a properly trained sales force (including dealers and consignees) at all times and to direct the execution of training programs.
6. To supervise programs for real estate acquisition, rebuilds; to evaluate the desirability of present service station locations; to recommend the most effective types of retail outlets for each locality.
7. To analyze and evaluate marketing station locations and recommend methods of operation.
8. To recommend and, where authorized, approve wages and salaries for Division personnel within policy limits.
9. To maintain civic, business, and off-the-job relations in such a manner as to maximize Union Oil Company's position in the community.
10. To contact personally key personnel of major accounts, both present and potential, so as to assist in selling activities and to maintain continuity of Union Oil relationships.
11. To direct Divisional Labor Relation efforts with the counsel of Home Office Staff.
12. To direct the efforts of the Divisional Personnel Manager in recruitment of personnel, training, and administration of employee benefit programs.

BRANCH SALES MANAGER
Acme Brick Company

[Because of changes in organizational structure, the following job description, current at the time the survey was taken, is no longer up to date. It is included because of its detailed outline of job responsibilities.]

PURPOSE: The Branch Manager is responsible for the effective direction and coordination of the salesmen and the Branch activities and the maintenance of good trade relationship in his area. He is to secure maximum dollar sales of the products in accordance with established sales policies and sales programs and within the limits of his expense budget.

AUTHORITY AND ORGANIZATIONAL RESPONSIBILITY

Reports to:
Division Sales Manager.

Supervises:
Salesmen.
Other Branch Office Personnel.

Functional Authority:
Develops effective working relationship with other Branch Managers, Plants, District Trucking Supervisor, Sales Coordinators, and General Office personnel so as to take full advantage of their help to achieve sales goals, reduce costs, and effectively carry out sales programs.

IMPORTANT DUTIES AND FUNCTIONS:

1. Directs the activities of the Branch; forecasts sales, expenses, manpower, and labor costs; and reviews the resulting budget with the Division Sales Manager for approval or revision.
2. Assigns salesmen to territories that have equitable workloads and that permit minimum travel costs so as to secure maximum dollar sales at minimum cost.
3. Sees to the complete and proper training of salesmen, including proper and effective sales techniques for various types of customers, recognizing the importance of all types.
4. Establishes and improves relationship at the Branch Office level with customers and others who influence the purchase of Company products.
5. Engages personally in active promotion and selling of all products and by this example and leadership adds substantially to the volume of business done by the Branch.
6. Engages in sales activities in support of salesmen and assists in maintaining and improving competitive position in handling special sales or competitive problems.
7. Recommends to the Division Sales Manager (for approval of Director of Marketing) changes in sales policies or prices as reflected by local or competitive situations.
8. Assumes the responsibility for efficient administration of the Branch operations in accordance with established policies and procedures.

9. Evaluates the performance of all Branch employees with the Division Sales Manager and recommends salary increases, promotions, and/or hiring of new employees.
10. Terminates employment of any salesman as needed, with the approval of the Division Sales Manager.
11. Terminates the employment of, and replaces, any clerical personnel on own authority.
12. Reviews and approves (with final approval by Division Sales Manager) salesmen's expense accounts and takes any necessary action to maintain a reasonable level of expense.
13. Authorizes all expenditures which have been approved in the Branch budget and forwards to the Division Sales Manager all other requests for expenditure.
14. Settles complaints as outlined in Section C, pages 6 and 7, of the *Marketing Procedure Manual*.
15. Approves credit on local orders and makes collections as necessary.
16. Maintains office facilities, services, and other Company property necessary to the conduct of Branch sales activities.
17. Sees that all Branch activities meet the Company and Department policies, procedures, and administration requirements.

These may be added where applicable:

A. Directs activities of Branch-based drivers and yard helpers.
B. Insures that safe conditions prevail at all work locations on Branch property.
C. Directs economical use of yard space consistent with prudent safety measures.
D. Operates sales yard with proper level of inventory to insure economical turnover and stockpiling of material.
E. Has responsibility to see to proper appearance of all Branch property.
F. Insures economical use of delivery time and equipment.
G. Assigns duties of unloading box cars so as to prevent demurrage costs.

MANAGER–SALES TRAINING
A Cosmetics Manufacturer

Basic Function: Establishes and operates training program for Zone Managers, salesmen, and trainees. Makes periodic field trips and conducts inside training sessions.

REPORTS TO Sales Manager. Has no direct supervisory responsibilities. Scope of position covers all Zone Managers, salesmen, and trainees in the Drugstore Sales Department.

DUTIES AND RESPONSIBILITIES

1. Continually travels to all zones of Drugstore Sales Department in country to work with salesmen to insure that Company's sales policies and programs are carried out. Accompanies salesmen and/or Zone Manager on sales calls and insures that all aspects of salesmen's performance are satisfactory.
2. Reports back to home office management on effectiveness of sales promotion material. Reports on sell-through of new products and competitors' products.
3. Plans formalized home office training sessions. Conducts sales classes.
4. Assists in planning and execution of sales meetings. May give training presentations at sales meetings.
5. Writes national bulletins on sales training, which are distributed to Area Managers, Zone Managers, and Assistant Zone Managers.
6. Writes and keeps salesmen's training manual current by making necessary revisions.
7. Reports on promotability of particular employees, or potential transferees, to home office management.
8. Plans and conducts special training schools and programs for sales trainees and Assistant Zone Managers. Constructs progress schedule for each group. Follows up on progress, for each trainee, by forms and reports. Answers and generates correspondence on training and development matters.
9. Trains supervisory personnel in hiring techniques. Sets hiring standards and assists in solving recruitment problems.
10. Designs forms of all types for salesmen's and Zone Managers' reporting and record keeping.
11. Designs salesmen's appraisal form and supervises semiannual evaluation and control of report.

MANAGER, SALES SERVICES
The Lufkin Rule Company

BASIC FUNCTION: Acts as customer contact regarding such matters as pricing, quality, scheduling, and shipping and insures prompt and efficient processing of customer orders and correspondence.

Responsibilities: The Manager, Sales Service, is responsible for

a. Handling orders, inquiries, editing, and pricing of the Sales Service Department.
b. Order-acknowledgment and tracer service.
c. Customer records and pricing of orders.
d. Returned goods, credits, claims, and adjustments of the Sales Department.
e. Performance and direction of the Manager, Special Sales–Tapes and Rules.
f. Assignment of personnel functioning in the aforementioned department.
g. Study and improvement of job methods and office routines in the Sales Department, including order handling, correspondence-incoming, and outgoing mail within this department.
h. Quoting prices and editing special and O.E.M. orders involving precision tools.
i. Serving as liaison between Sales and other departments where information or clarification is necessary to properly handle customer correspondence or orders.
j. Editing and establishing prices for precision-tool parts price list.
k. Keeping Sales Manager current on problems in Sales Service Department.

Relationship

a. Reports to Sales Manager.
b. Provides advice and guidance to those outside his department in areas of his responsibility, on his own initiative or by request.
c. Coordinates his activities with other members of Management on matters of mutual concern, and is guided by them on matters within their provinces.
d. Reporting directly to Manager, Sales Service:
   (1) Sales Service Salesmen.
   (2) Record Clerk.
   (3) Tracer Clerk-Typist.
   (4) Order Acknowledgment, Tracer and Sales Expediter Clerk.
   (5) Credit Claim and Adjustment Clerk.
   (6) Manager, Special Sales–Tapes and Rules.

DIRECTOR–PRODUCT DEVELOPMENT
The Quaker Oats Company

Reports to: Group Vice President, Corporate Development

ACCOUNTABILITY OBJECTIVE

To establish amounts and priorities for capital expenditures and R&D efforts in support of new products in existing product areas; to recommend and implement development of products in areas in which Quaker has no entries and to coordinate activities of all departments involved in product development.

NATURE AND SCOPE

The incumbent evaluates proposed Grocery Products R&D projects to advise on which projects should be authorized and given what priority. Some of the important criteria considered in establishing project priority are the project's relation to current and proposed work; its chance of success, from both an R&D and a marketing standpoint; its potential for both long- and short-range profit contribution. Once projects are approved, the incumbent coordinates and expedites development efforts of the various activities involved. The incumbent's involvement with R&D projects continues until the product is marketed nationally. Selection of projects with the best potential is complicated by the large number of proposals that must be analyzed; up to 200 projects may be up for approval at any given time. The probable success of a proposed project is based on past experience with similar projects, advice from Barrington R&D, market conditions, Commercial Research tests, cost factors, etc.

He directs the marketing and financial evaluation of all capital expenditures for additional volume or new products.

He is responsible for evaluating areas outside those in which the Company currently has products and for recommending product areas for development. He initiates the necessary marketing research to identify product attributes and authorizes R&D effort. He works closely with Product Management, Manufacturing, Commercial Research, Engineering, various areas of the Controller's Department, etc.

Since the position deals with proposals that will have a future impact on company profits, it demands foresight, objectivity, analytical ability, and imagination. Expediting projects is important, and the incumbent must therefore be capable of motivating management personnel. Intimate knowledge of corporate products, marketing approaches, accounting procedures, and production methods is vital. Ten to fifteen years' exposure to production and product management activities (including supervisory positions) is required for adequate background experience.

The incumbent reports to the Group Vice President, Corporate Development, as does the Vice President, Research and Development, as does the Director of Corporate Planning, Burry Division and Wolf Brand Products.

The following positions report directly to the incumbent: 6 Product Development Managers (Cereals and Snacks, 2; Mixes and Frozen, Corn Goods, Industrial and Institutional, 1; Pet Foods, 2); New Areas (1); one secretary. Product Development Managers are chosen from all functional areas of the Corporation as a result of above-average achievement. During the two or three years they remain in Product Development they are given intensive training by the incumbent to better prepare them for broadened responsibilities in other departments.

The incumbent is free to advise management on product development without clearing the advice with his immediate superior. However, deviations from established policies must be approved by the Vice President.

DIMENSIONS

Personnel count in the suborganization: 12 salaried.
Approximate annual expenditure on R&D and new capital: $_____.
Equipment necessitated by R&D activity: _____.
F'68 New Product Sales: $_____.

PRINCIPAL ACCOUNTABILITIES

1. To authorize, coordinate, assign priority, and expedite R&D projects to assure efficient handling of projects.
2. To recommend for development product areas in which Quaker has no entries (and establish criteria for development) to contribute to profitable expansion of marketing activities. To develop appropriate products in these areas.
3. To communicate with management and other departments regarding R&D and capital expenditures for new products.
4. To establish and administer procedures for improving efficiency of product development efforts to assure full value for the research dollar.
5. To motivate and train subordinates to assure effective staff support and to prepare subordinates for broadened responsibilities.
6. To prepare written recommendations on specific projects for the Executive Committee in order to obtain approval for capital expenditures and/or R&D funds.
7. To conduct a monthly New Product Meeting and administer preparation of the accompanying report to inform all involved personnel of product development activity.

DIRECTOR OF MARKETING SERVICES
The Glidden Company

[Because of changes in organization structure at The Glidden Company, the following job description is no longer current. It is included because of its detailed outline of job responsibilities.]

REPORTS TO: Vice President, Coatings and Resins Group

BASIC FUNCTION: To plan, direct, control, administer and coordinate programs in market research, advertising, sales promotion and merchandising for all Group sales which will maximize the timely and effective marketing of the products of the Coatings and Resins Group.

NATURE AND SCOPE

Under the direction of the Vice President, C & R Group, the incumbent is responsible for providing total market services pertaining to market research, advertising, sales promotion and merchandising of all Glidden products sold directly or through district centers, branches, leased departments, dealers or wholesalers.

These areas of service under specific direction of managers are responsible for accomplishing the following activities:

Market Research—provides the means for analyzing market findings and discovering new areas for sales development, compilation of information on total market opportunity, sales account analysis, obtaining information concerning salability of all products, and analysis and coordination of specific and general marketing services. Approximately 20 percent of Corporate Research time is utilized to fulfill these responsibilities.

Advertising and Color—is responsible for the creation and production of all advertising media which implements sales programs; the planning, budgeting and developing of publication advertising for Trade Sales Maintenance and Industrial Divisions; and the implementation of advertising agency ideas.

A staff of seventeen (17) employees carry out the responsibilities of creation and production of all media, leaving specialization to the Color Studio and Color Laboratory.

Nine (9) employees in the Color Studio provide color presentations and color schemes to aid our sales representatives in selling customers requiring such services. Additionally, they assist the Advertising staff on color trends and color-card layout.

Under the Director, Color Department, three (3) employees in the Color Laboratory provide the formulation and control of color standards, special panels for industrial products, and the development of color systems.

Because of the complexities and variety of advertising stock, warehousing and distribution of these materials have been centralized under a single location and control operating within the bounds of a sound and well-planned budget. The efforts of three employees and two additional part-time employees are required.

Retailing—is responsible for retail programs, budgets, coordination, anp communication of retail activities, including retail training, testing, field surveys, and audits. This also includes the development of In-Home Selling Programs and evaluation of their profitability.

Retail Advertising and Promotion—is responsible for planning; reviewing; and analyzing retail advertising, promotion, signing and display, and miscellaneous retail and dealer advertising needs and special feature advertising. There is also the responsibility of procuring advertising space, layout and copy for Leased Departments.

Sales Promotion—encompasses the responsibility for Shows, Conventions, Exhibits, Point of Sale Displays and Ad-Merchandising Programs; provides C & R Group communications through Trade Sales and Dealer Newsletters, dealer promotional calendars and promotional activities; and acts as liaison between Trade Sales Maintenance, Industrial Sales and the Advertising Departments, as well as on special regional promotions and market tests.

In conjunction with these activities the incumbent directs the preparation, implementation and control of annual advertising and promotional budgets in coordination with the Group Vice President and Vice President, Marketing, and the General Manager, Industrial Sales.

Because of the many services which are required of our advertising agency, he maintains liaison between the agency and our Advertising, Branch Retailing and Leased Department staffs to coordinate local-national advertising, merchandising and allied activities.

Additionally, his responsibilities involve budgets and advertising agency activities of C & R International units; test marketing of Gates Engineering and Macco Division products; creation and layout of labels; coordination of Sales, Advertising and other departments in design and development of new packaging; planning and coordination of all national sales meetings;

and analyzing effectiveness of market service programs of proposed acquisitions.

He is a member of the C & R Trade Sales Product Planning, C & R Group Long-Range Planning and C & R Group Management Committees.

ACCOUNTABILITIES

1. Achieve the objectives established for national marketing services, advertising, promotional and publicity programs, within the limits of prescribed budgets, including review and control of both national and local budgets.
2. Maintain and develop subordinates for continued effectiveness of departmental functions.
3. Develop efficient methods of review and analysis to measure impact and profitability of marketing service and advertising programs.
4. Ensure continued improvement and sophistication of marketing service and advertising procedures and methods.
5. Ensure that marketing services and advertising objectives will complement and enhance general overall C & R Group objectives.

GENERAL MARKETING ADMINISTRATOR
Cessna Aircraft Company

ORGANIZATIONAL RELATIONSHIP

Line: Reports to: Vice President–Marketing, Commercial Aircraft

Supervises: Marketing Planning Manager
     Division Controller
     Business Management Manager
     Personnel and Procedures Manager
     Manager–Merchandising and Training

Staff: Advises, assists, and cooperates with all department and division heads and their personnel in the administration and coordination of all Division activities.

PRIMARY FUNCTION:

Administer and coordinate Division activities; supervise financial affairs and accounting functions for the Division; supervise scheduling of aircraft orders and assist in planning production requirements; supervise the personnel program and the policies and procedures used in the Division; supervise the merchandising activities and the training activities of the Division; and supervise the business management program, through the regional sales organization, for the distributor and dealer organization; and assist in preparing the objectives of the Marketing Division.

Specific Duties:

1. Administers and coordinates Marketing Division activities as specified by the Vice President–Marketing, Commercial Aircraft.
2. Supervises the handling of all financial affairs of the Division and supplies division and corporate management with pertinent financial data.
3. Is responsible for the accounting activities of the Division.
4. Oversees the forecast of aircraft order receipts, assists in scheduling production to fill orders, processes the order receipt, and coordinates delivery of aircraft.
5. Supervises the personnel activities for the Division.
6. Is responsible for developing, maintaining and disseminating Division internal policies and procedures and those of the Company affecting all distributors and dealers.
7. Supervises the business management program, through the regional sales organization, for assisting the distributor and dealer organizations.
8. Supervises the Marketing Division Merchandising programs and Marketing Division Training programs for assisting the General Sales Department in the merchandising of Marketing Division products and the sales and service training of distributor and dealer organizations.
9. Coordinates preparation of the detailed marketing plan in support of the Long-Range Plan.
10. Coordinates with other Marketing Staff members as required to assist them in carrying out their responsibilities and in meeting the marketing objectives contained in both short- and long-range planning.
11. Supervises the customer relations program for all visitors to Company headquarters in Wichita.
12. Is responsible for liaison with the Company's legal counsel on all matters affecting the marketing of commercial aircraft and parts.
13. Supervises office services of printing, mail room, equipment maintenance, janitorial duties, local transportation and scheduling of resident aircraft.
14. Organizes the work of his group in such a manner as to provide his subordinates with growth opportunity and latitude in decision making as steps in their development. In this connection, plans objectives and goals for the group, delegates responsibility and commensurate au-

thority and periodically evaluates the performance of his subordinates in their assigned tasks.

15. Travels to the field occasionally for direct contact with dealers, distributors and customers and attends national meetings and conventions.
16. Prepares replies to correspondence received in his areas of responsibility.

MANAGER–INTERNATIONAL DIVISION
Univis, Inc.

REPORTING RELATIONSHIP: The Manager–International Division reports directly to the Vice President for Marketing.

GENERAL RESPONSIBILITY: The Manager–International Division is primarily responsible for the sales of current company products, as well as obsolete company products, in international markets. He is responsible for recommending policies governing direct and indirect international sales and service and possible imports, including pricing, promotion and advertising, packaging, transportation and credit. He is responsible for making periodic visits to important international markets to expand the Univis base of operations. He is also responsible for developing international trade which could be beneficial to the Company.

DUTIES: In carrying out his general responsibility the Manager–International Division performs the following duties:
1. Supervises the development, installation and administration of methods, procedures and facilities required to accomplish objectives and programs.
2. Supervises international sales activities and possible import activities.
3. Is responsible for meeting established international sales quotas and submitting periodic reports in conjunction with same.
4. Directs sales surveys to determine market potentials.
5. Develops, in conjunction with the Advertising Manager, international advertising programs and suitable domestic advertising in international markets.
6. Assists in the development of new international products for export and possible import products.
7. Arranges for visits of international distributors to Univis plants.
8. Makes periodic visits to important international markets.

9. Cooperates with industry groups directly interested in international trade.
10. Assists in the development of special unit packaging required for specific markets.
11. Prepares, in conjunction with the Market Research Department, estimates of international sales.
12. Recommends improvements in existing products, where desirable, to meet competitive or other conditions.
13. Assists in the negotiation of licensing arrangements for overseas manufacturers.
14. Coordinates planning and timing and recommends pricing to sell these products at optimum price.
15. Sells these products at prices approved by the Vice President for Marketing.
16. Provides to the Vice President for Marketing, both informally and in report form, statements of results achieved against departmental programs and budgets.

Scope and Limits of Authority: The Manager–International Division has authority derived from the Vice President for Marketing. He plans, organizes, directs, coordinates and controls the activities of his division. He is limited in the exercise of this authority in the following ways:

1. Current established Company objectives, policies, programs and procedures set limits on current department activities.
2. Changes in objectives, policies, programs or procedures which affect in any way the operations of another department or division must be cleared by the Vice President for Marketing.
3. Authorized marketing plan as approved by the Executive Committee.
4. Authorized price lists as approved by the Executive Committee.
5. Employment, promotion, transfer and release of supervisors and staff personnel are limited by approved organization plan.
6. Compensation of supervisory and nonsupervisory personnel is limited by pay policy, with any exception therefrom to be approved by the Executive Committee.

Index by Company Name

Index by Job Description